THE INSTITUTE OF POLITICS PUBLICATIONS
WILLIAMS COLLEGE, WILLIAMSTOWN, MASS.

THE REAWAKENING OF THE ORIENT
AND OTHER ADDRESSES

THE
REAWAKENING OF THE ORIENT
AND OTHER ADDRESSES

BY
SIR VALENTINE CHIROL
YUSUKE TSURUMI
SIR JAMES ARTHUR SALTER

NEW HAVEN
PUBLISHED FOR THE INSTITUTE OF POLITICS
BY THE YALE UNIVERSITY PRESS
LONDON · HUMPHREY MILFORD · OXFORD UNIVERSITY PRESS
MCMXXV

CONTENTS

I. THE REAWAKENING OF THE ORIENT

II. THE GREAT INDIAN EXPERIMENT

BY SIR VALENTINE CHIROL

I

THE REAWAKENING OF THE ORIENT

WHEN I first heard the East a-calling to me, now, I regret to say, nearly fifty years ago, the enduring supremacy of the Occident over the Orient was almost universally assumed as a matter of course. The Western nations claimed it in virtue of their superior civilization, and were able to enforce it by their superior material and economic equipment. The peoples of the Orient themselves seemed to accept it, in spite of spasms of revolt, with the fatalistic resignation which was then supposed to be their chief characteristic. The Turk, who had once stood before the gates of Vienna, was regarded as a sick man, doomed to disappear before long from Europe, and the only question at issue was the division of his inheritance between rival European powers and the Christian subject races in European Turkey, whose deep sense of nationhood had never been wholly stifled by century-long enslavement. Morocco was still an independent Mohammedan kingdom, in a forgotten corner of northwest Africa, and most of the other lands of the ancient Arab Khalifate were still nominally incorporated with the Ottoman Empire, though the annexation of Algeria by France had already driven in a deep wedge between Morocco and Tunis. Egypt was still an autonomous province of Turkey, though the profligate extravagance of the rulers of Egypt was hurrying on the introduction of foreign financial and political control which culminated a few years later in the British occupation of the Nile

Valley. Persia and Afghanistan counted for little except as buffer states between the British and the Russian Empires in Asia. Queen Victoria was on the point of assuming the title of Empress of India as the crowning symbol of British dominion in an Asiatic subcontinent, peopled by nearly a fifth of the whole human race. China and Japan will not come within my purview, as I only propose to deal with those parts of the Orient whose history has been far longer and more closely interlocked with that of the Occident. I will merely say that half a century ago they were barely emerging from the self-imposed isolation in which they had been content to live their own separate lives, cut off from all contact with the outer world, until the Occident went and thundered at their gates demanding admission in a voice that would take no denial. No one realized then, I think, that however reluctantly Japan had been dragged out of her ancient seclusion into the fierce conflicts of a world hitherto unknown to her, she was already quite determined to play the part of hammer rather than of anvil. Nor did anyone foresee the mighty stirring of deep waters which China's unwilling contact with the Occident was ultimately to produce, with consequences still far beyond our ken.

How vastly different is the spectacle which the Orient today presents, from the Atlantic shores of Morocco through northern Africa and right across Asia to the far-off coast of the Pacific. All along that far-flung line its people are being roused from a long, lethargic sleep by the masterful impact of the Occident itself. They have begun to question and to probe and to challenge Western supremacy, intellectual and spiritual, economic and material. They are resuscitating memories, sometimes quite mythical, of former greatness and legends of a long-forgotten nationhood. They are rallying the dormant forces of ancient and deep-seated civilizations—sometimes more ancient than our own—and still vital. They are refurbishing the armor of militant faiths with a religious fervor which the Occident has long outgrown. They are borrowing new weapons, even from the Occident's own arsenal and invoking against it its vaunted principles of nationalism and self-determination.

This reawakening of the Orient assumes a different shape in different countries. But there is one feature common to all. They belong to many different races, and have different religious and social systems, but they are all united in a common resentment of the white man's assumption of superiority and of indefeasible rights based on the superiority of a race which owes to nature a generally lighter complexion than that of the population of the Orient. Never before has the white man stressed the color-bar as he does today as the rampart of his racial superiority. Never before has the Orient denied his claim to racial superiority so emphatically as it does today. It denies it sometimes with all the fierceness of atavistic instincts revived by the clash of conflicting civilizations and religions—sometimes contemptuously, because increasing intercourse has bred familiarity with the seamy side of Occidental civilization—sometimes, but, unfortunately, more rarely, because the Oriental has assimilated enough of the finer spirit of the Occident to demand equal partnership for itself in all that is best of it.

Absorbed as we are in the many anxious problems

which the Great War and the peace settlements have bequeathed to us, we are often, I think, apt to overlook, or to underrate, the grave dangers with which this reawakening of the Orient confronts the whole human race, unless some way be found to a peaceful readjustment of relations between the Occident and the Orient before the world shall have been plunged into deadly racial conflict. Bitter as are their present-day discords, the Western nations all move, roughly speaking, on the same plane of civilization. And herein should lie the best assurance of ultimate reconciliation and peace. It is quite otherwise with the Orient. Behind its angry discontent there is the surge of many Old World forces, often, it is true, in conflict with each other, but tending more and more to combine together against the common menace of the Occident.

It is the Reawakening of the Orient, and I call it so advisedly. For it must not be forgotten that there was a long period in history when the Orient was itself more dynamic than the Occident, when the Arabs who poured forth out of the Arabian desert with the Koran in one hand and the sword in the other swept right through Spain and into the very heart of France, and when again the Turks stood before the walls of Vienna less than two and a half centuries ago. The vital energy supplied to the Orient by the one great world religion which was born armed with the sword seems to have spent itself in those two mighty efforts. For the great Saracenic civilization which the Arab conquerors at least evolved whilst Europe was plunged in the darkness of our Middle Ages perished with the advent of the Turk, who, with an infinite capacity for destruction, has never been

able to construct. The new culture of the Italian Ren-
aissance, on the other hand, heralded the enfranchisement of the Occident from medieval darkness. The
field of human knowledge was steadily enlarged.
Modern Europe grew vital whilst the Orient stood
still. The organized application of improved and increasingly scientific methods under the pressure of
new economic needs gave the Occident a new driving
power unknown to the Orient.

But it was the economic pressure of the Turk upon
Europe when his power was at its apogee that precipitated the great discovery which suddenly opened
the way for the Occident's intrusion upon the Orient.
The Turk knew it not. He understood nothing about
economic pressure. He believed only in the power of
his sword. The vast empire which his sword once
conquered has crumbled away, but the one service he
ever rendered to the world remains, though now almost forgotten—namely, that by closing to Western
trade its old overland rights of way to the Orient he
drove Europe to explore the ocean for new highways
and to discover America just when she did, and to
find by the same token a hitherto untraveled road
over the seas to India, where no European invader
had set foot since Alexander the Great, until the Portuguese, having rounded the Cape of Good Hope,
landed eighteen centuries later on its southwestern
shores.

The same economic forces that had driven the
Occident to turn the land barrier by which the Turk
had closed the Orient against it and overcome the
more mysterious barrier of wide oceans, plunged the
Western nations into a prolonged struggle amongst
themselves for the new markets opened up to them in

the Orient. Nowhere was the struggle fiercer than in India, and if the British were not first in the field, they outfought and outstayed their rivals, Portuguese and Spaniards, Dutchmen and French; and they ultimately stayed there, no longer merely or chiefly to trade, but to carry out over a much longer period and on a far larger scale than anything ever attempted elsewhere, a tremendous experiment of government and administration on a huge and remote subcontinent of Asia, the success or failure of which may show whether it is really possible to bring the Orient into the orbit of Western civilization. To that experiment my second chapter will be devoted. I shall deal today with the emergence of a Turkish Republic and of a new Egyptian state in the lands which have been from time immemorial the meeting place and the battleground of Occident and Orient.

The possession of India, which, it must be remembered, made England a great Asiatic power just when, owing to the American War of Independence, she ceased to be the dominant power in this continent, necessarily led to a great change in the orientation of her whole foreign policy. It was governed throughout the greater part of the nineteenth century by the growing rivalry between Great Britain and Russia, both by that time great Asiatic as well as European powers, and both jealous and distrustful of each other—at a time, too, when the Ottoman Empire, having ceased to be a menace to Europe, offered in its decrepitude an irresistible temptation to the ambitions of all the chief European powers. This assistance was invoked by its Christian subject races who were stirred once more by the sense of independent nationhood which centuries of enslavement had never wholly stifled; and with its great natural resources, which the Turk was incapable of developing, it presented a wide field for Western exploitation, when steam and electricity were transforming the economic life of the Occident.

In the struggle between Russia, who wanted to wipe Turkey off the map of Europe as an incurable plague spot, and England, who vainly hoped to make her reform her ways and to preserve her as a bulwark against the menace of Russian expansion towards India, the balance of power played on the whole a larger part than any definite economic purpose. In defense of his position as a Mohammedan ruling race, and as the last great Mohammedan power in the world, the Turk still knew how to fight and even became a past-master in the art of diplomatic intrigue, which he rapidly learned from the Occident, and which was about the only thing he ever learned. But he more readily succumbed to the fatal facilities which contact with modern methods of finance afforded to the reckless extravagance of a seldom economically-minded Orient. He was beaten in war and humiliated in peace by constantly renewed threats of coercion, but the money markets of Europe contributed largely to his undoing. Only in the last part of the nineteenth century did the strange and sinister genius of the Sultan Abdul Hamid II conceive a great scheme for retrieving the territorial losses to which his Empire had been subjected, by reviving and extending far beyond the frontiers of his temporal dominion, the spiritual authority with which he claimed to be invested over all orthodox Mohammedans as Khalif of Islam. He created the Turkish Pan-Islamic movement, which survived his own downfall in 1908,

and, England having at last come to the conclusion
that she had backed the wrong horse when she fought
the Crimean War in 1854 and again went to the verge
of war against Russia to defend Turkey in 1878, he
found a powerful ally in Germany, who, in the full
tide of her industrial and commercial expansion, was
ready to throw her mantle over the Red Sultan in
return for the Baghdad Railway and many other
scarcely less valuable concessions which were to pave
the way for her economic domination over Turkey.
William II himself aimed at far more, for soon after
his accession he told Bismarck that for him Turkey
was going to be the bridgehead to German world
domination. In vain did the old chancellor observe
that the term "world dominion" did not figure in his
political dictionary. He was dismissed for his pains,
and William II pursued as elsewhere the headstrong
policy which led to the World War.

By the Turkish revolution of 1908, though it was
primarily a military revolt engineered by a number
of young and ambitious officers, the government of
the Ottoman Empire was transferred to a group of
men, known as the Committee of Union and Progress,
many of whom had been banished as dangerously
liberal-minded under Abdul Hamid II, of whose despotic régime delation and corruption were the two
chief pillars. The Committee professed, at first, to
inaugurate a new régime of "liberty, justice, and fra-
ternity" on approved Occidental lines. But even
during the exuberant honeymoon which for a short
time united all the races and the creeds of the Ottoman Empire, the Union and Progress men never
committed themselves to the word "equality." Their
religion—and they were not all Mohammedans—sat

lightly upon them, and though they kept Pan-Islam-
ism in reserve, as a second string to their bow, their
policy was mainly inspired by a fierce and intolerant
nationalism directed in the first place to the maintenance of the absolute supremacy of the Turkish ruling race over non-Turkish Mohammedans as well as
Christians throughout the Ottoman Empire itself,
and then to the establishment of Turkish hegemony
outside the Turkish Empire over all the peoples of
the Orient whose affinity to the Turks could be argued
on any grounds, however remote, of history or language or descent.

This was the Pan-Turanian movement which was
carried to such lengths during the Great War that
its protagonists revived the use of the pagan war-
cries and emblems of the primitive Turkish tribes in
their far-off pre-Mohammedan days. The Armenian
massacres of 1916, carried out in Asia Minor under
the direct orders of the two supreme war leaders,
Enver Pasha, the Minister of War, and Talaat
Pasha, the Minister of the Interior, on a far larger
scale and with far greater thoroughness than Abdul
Hamid had ever dared, were the by-products of Pan-
Turanianism, and though its wilder dreams were
shattered by the final overthrow of Turkey and her
Allies in the Great War, Turkish nationalism retained
sufficient vitality to produce the sudden militant resurgence of Turkey which has driven the Greeks out
of Asia Minor and imposed upon the powers of
western Europe the sacrifice of almost all their
earlier war aims in the final Treaty of Lausanne.

Turkish nationalism, however, did not owe that
diplomatic triumph merely or even chiefly to its facile
victories over the Greek armies hopelessly demoral-

ized and reduced to the most miserable straits by King Constantine's incompetent ministers at Athens. It owed it partly to Mohammedan demonstrations of Pan-Islamic sympathy outside Turkey, and notably in India, which had a great influence on British policy. It owed it still more to the old jealousies between the Allies themselves. The French, and less openly the Italians, succumbed to the old lure of economic concessions which the men of Angora held out to them. The British people were utterly war-weary and their Prime Minister, Mr. Lloyd George, whose influence had at first prevailed upon the Allies to mobilize Greece against the recalcitrant Turks in Asia Minor, had not the honesty or the courage to tell the Greeks that the encouragement which he continued to give them behind the backs of his own Allies, whilst they were encouraging the Turks behind his back, was merely the expression of his own personal and perfectly futile good will. But in the intoxication of victory the Turk was only moved to persevere still further in a fanatical reversion to the primitive tribalism of the Central Asian hordes that are his forebears. Turkish nationalism has been carried in effect to such lengths that it has not only savagely rid its soil of all alien races at the imminent risk of economic suicide, but it has also cut itself adrift from the brotherhood of Islam by the abolition of the Ottoman Khalifate as well as of the Ottoman Sultanate, in order to dig itself in the more securely against all contact with the non-Turkish Orient as well as with the Occident. How far Turkey will have gained by the substitution of a lay republic which is the very negation of Islam for the theocratic state which Abdul Hamid's Pan-Islamic policy had once sought to revive, one is at a loss to see. The Khalifate may be dead in Turkey, but it is an Islamic and not merely a Turkish institution and may be resuscitated elsewhere and used, not as it has been recently and with great effect, to the political advantage of Turkey, but against her.

What does the new Turkish state amount to? According to the American Relief Committee, a quarter of the whole population of the Ottoman Empire perished between 1914 and the end of the Great War from war casualties, disease, starvation, and massacre. Today the population of the Turkish Republic is estimated at some seven or at most eight millions. It is doubtless a more homogeneous population than it ever was before. For of the Greeks and Armenians who in 1914 still numbered over three millions in Asia Minor, only the scantiest remnants are left. They constituted the most intelligent and economically valuable element in the country, and the Turk has rooted them out. The European settlements, which also played their very important part in the economic development of the country, have lost, by the abolition of the capitulations under the Treaty of Lausanne, the permanent safeguards which all Occidental powers had hitherto deemed essential for the security of foreign life and property in a state where justice, as administered in Turkish law courts, has hitherto been and still is a byword. Hostility to all foreigners except privileged travelers and a few correspondents whom it is thought useful to try to cajole, has never been so deliberately and insolently displayed as it is today, when the whole machinery of administration is centralized at Angora, where the

Turk thinks himself safe from all possible forms of external pressure.

The New Turkey has not formally repudiated its old financial obligations abroad as Soviet Russia has done, but in practice she is already ignoring them. Yet she can be saved from absolute bankruptcy only by restoring her shattered credit abroad, and this she can do only by surrendering to Western capitalists the exploitation of her great natural resources, which she is more incapable than ever of developing for herself now that she has deprived herself of the use of Greek and Armenian brains. If Turkey's financial necessities compel her to revive the offers of concessions by which she bribed M. Franklin-Bouillon to conclude the Angora agreement which she has hitherto treated as a mere scrap of paper, can she be kept to them? If she doesn't keep to them, will the door not be reopened to the various forms of foreign intervention against which her intense nationalism rebels? The Treaty of Lausanne has restored not only Constantinople and the Straits to her, but a large slice of Thrace. She is still a European power, though her rulers are afraid to return to Constantinople. How long will the Balkan States, who twelve years ago, in one of the rare moments in which their higher common interests prevailed over their narrow and selfish jealousies, very nearly succeeded in driving her out of Europe, be content to leave her there? How long will Bolshevist Russia, who has already reverted to the Tsarist policy of military domination in the Caucasus and in Central Asia, maintain with Turkey the intimate relations of amity which drew them together when Angora and Moscow were both at war with western Europe? How long will even the dictatorship of Mustapha Kemal Pasha endure? He was the only leader who emerged from the welter of corruption and incompetence at Constantinople during the Great War with clean hands and a high reputation of military ability and powers of organization, and the Turkish Grand National Assembly has been the creation and so far the docile instrument of his masterful will. But even some of his followers are already displaying signs of restiveness, and it has yet to be proved that the revolution by which Mustapha Kemal has torn the Turkish people from their old Mohammedan moorings, corresponds as fully as his friends would have us believe with any fundamental change in the psychology or temper of the Turk, who has always destroyed but never built.

The thorny question of the Mosul province, which Turkey still claims to recover from Mesopotamia, has not yet been settled, and if she cannot come to an agreement with England it is to be referred to the League of Nations. That may possibly prove to be the acid test of Turkish good faith under the Treaty of Lausanne. But Turkish nationalism also makes the recovery of Mosul the acid test of its rulers' patriotism. Turkey has indeed reawakened, but has her reawakening conduced, or is it likely to conduce, to a peaceful readjustment of the relations between the Orient and the Occident?

Can one speak more confidently of the reawakening of the Orient in Egypt? The ancient land of the Pharaohs, never again independent after the Persian conquest in 500 B.C., passed for nearly three centuries into complete oblivion after the blight of Turkish domination fell upon it in 1517. It was in the hope of dealing a deadly blow at England's position in the

East and with an eye even to the future conquest of
India that Bonaparte embarked upon his meteoric
expedition to Egypt in the last year of the eighteenth
century and drew her into the maelstrom of European political and economic rivalries. England, in
open alliance then for the first time with Turkey,
drove Bonaparte out of Egypt, but another soldier
of fortune, Mohammed Ali, who had landed with the
Turkish army as a captain of Albanian auxiliaries,
remained, and out of the chaos which had resulted
from the first conflict of European arms on Egyptian
soil he leaped into the saddle as a Turkish governor,
and then twice rebelled against his Turkish suzerain
in a prolonged struggle for Egyptian independence.
His victorious armies twice threatened the existence
of the Ottoman Empire. But though he had the sympathy and encouragement of France, England, re-
membering Bonaparte, was alarmed for the safety
of her communications with India, and, with the
coöperation of other but more lukewarm powers,
thought to checkmate France by coercing Mohammed
Ali into submission to his Turkish suzerain, who,
however, granted him hereditary rights as Pasha of
Egypt with a very large measure of autonomy. Mohammed Ali was a great barbarian, and, though his
one supreme ambition was foiled and though his
methods were crude and tyrannical, he laid the foun-
dations of modern Egypt by promoting Western
education, by encouraging Western trade, by intro-
ducing Western industries, by establishing public
security throughout the country, and, with consequences which he perhaps little foresaw, by developing the Overland Route to India, even at a time when
British policy was by no means friendly to him.

The contact thus established between Egypt and the Occident was then for some time mainly economic. A large inflow of Europeans, unfortunately not always of the best type, discovered that there were still highly attractive fleshpots in Egypt. The American Civil War gave Egypt her chance to become a great cotton-growing country when the rapidly expanding cotton industries of Europe found themselves suddenly deprived of their American raw material. The use of steam power on sea as well as on land restored Egypt to her ancient position as a highway between Europe and the more remote parts of the Orient. The construction of railways between Alexandria and Suez enabled England to rush troops to India during the Mutiny of 1857. She entirely failed at first to recognize the commercial value of the scheme revived by the great Frenchman, Ferdinand de Lesseps, for the construction of a ship canal between the Mediterranean and the Red Sea, and Palmerston, partly from mere political jealousy of France, fought a long and stubborn fight against it; but the Suez Canal was built and opened in 1869 and rapidly became one of the great arteries of British world trade and of Britain's naval communications with many of her chief oversea possessions.

But there was another side to the picture of Egypt's growing intimacy with the Occident. Mohammed Ali's successors inherited none of his rugged qualities but a good deal of his ambitious and despotic temperament, and on a much lower plane. They surrounded themselves with European adventurers and flatterers recruited from the large foreign communities of all nationalities that had been drawn to Egypt by the commercial and industrial opportunities which the general growth of material wealth afforded. These communities enjoyed the protection of the separate consular jurisdiction established of old throughout the Ottoman Empire under the treaty system of Capitulations, which granted them many special privileges even in the matter of taxation. Each community thus grew into a small *imperium in imperio,* curtailing and sometimes altogether paralyzing the Egyptian executive and administrative authority. The consuls used and abused their powers in the furtherance of the political purposes which their governments were pursuing. Yet notwithstanding the spread of Western education, still very superficial, amongst the official and well-to-do classes, the Egyptians took no active part in the development of the economic life of their country, which they left entirely to these foreign communities, and down to the present day very few Egyptians, if any, have emerged as captains of industry or commerce or finance. Foreigners, on the other hand, built up large industrial and commercial and financial interests, and, though some of them did so on perfectly sound and legitimate lines and to the real benefit of Egypt, many of the baser sort were chiefly concerned to extract fat concessions or lucrative orders from the Egyptian rulers, which often served merely as a pretext for building up huge claims for compensation to be recovered under cover of the Capitulations and by dint of diplomatic pressure.

The climax was reached, in the 70's of the last century, under the Khedive Ismail, who bought his new-fangled title as ruler of Egypt from the Sultan of Turkey by a colossal personal bribe. He grafted the indulgence of the most profligate tastes borrowed

from the Occident onto the most ruthless methods of
Oriental despotism. If he filched from his subjects
fully a quarter of the best lands in the valley of the
Nile, that was merely straining an Oriental practice.
It was as a reckless borrower on the European money
markets that he struck out a new and for all Oriental
peoples a most dangerous line. The financiers of Paris
and London received him with open arms, for the
credit of the Egyptian state seemed to be ample.
European money poured in, and Ismail spent it
chiefly on his own pleasures, on his palaces and his
harems, on the pomp and circumstance of a court
which, he fondly imagined, rivaled that of a European sovereign's, on futile armaments and vast
schemes of aggrandizement in Abyssinia and Central Africa. It was the Oriental Rake's Progress,
and it showed even more clearly than what happened at the same time in Turkey, how dangerous for
an Oriental state are the facilities which modern
financial methods afford to the mad extravagance
common to so many Oriental rulers. There was a limit
to the golden eggs which Egypt could lay. It was soon
reached. Her creditors grew exacting. Ismail mort-
gaged his own property as recklessly as that of the
state, if indeed he ever discriminated between the
two. When he could no longer borrow from the great
European banks, he borrowed from local foreign
usurers and on increasingly ruinous terms. The
wretched Egyptian peasant, on whose shoulders the
whole burden ultimately rested, was bled white. He
was made to pay his taxes for years ahead and often
twice and thrice over; he was forced to sell his stand-
ing crops at derisive prices to the tame money lender
whom the tax gatherer carried round with him; he

was dragged away in chains from his own fields (this I saw with my own eyes) to work under the overseer's whip on the Khedive's huge personal estates. The end came in 1879, when Ismail was deposed at the instance of France and England, who at once introduced a rigid financial control over Egyptian expenditure in the interest of Egypt herself no less than of her bondholders abroad.

England and France could plead that it was the only means of saving Egypt from bankruptcy and chaos, but their action gave international finance for the first time a lever which it has used more and more frequently ever since, and often with less justification, and not only in the Orient.

The misery into which Ismail had plunged the Egyptian people was intense and in their despair they were unable to discriminate between the oppression of their own rulers or the greed of the bondholders in the background and the somewhat severe discipline of the foreign administrators brought in to extricate them from the morass in which all were floundering. Out of their inarticulate resentment, and a revival at the same time of the old undercurrent of Mohammedan hostility to all European influences, grew up a first but very feeble nationalist movement in Egypt under Arabi, the Egyptian, which culminated in a revolt of the Egyptian army against Ismail's well-meaning but feeble successor, the Khedive Tewfik. A murderous anti-foreign outbreak at Alexandria rendered European intervention inevitable, and as none would join with England to bell the Egyptian cat, a British army was landed in Egypt in the summer of 1882 and has remained there ever since.

England did not annex Egypt, as it might have meant a dangerous breach with France, nor was even a British Protectorate then proclaimed. A halfway house was found in a system of British control, under which the Khedive's authority and the Egyptian framework of indigenous administration were preserved, as well as the international status of Egypt as an autonomous province of the Ottoman Empire, but the one real driving and directing power remained in the hands of the British representative in Cairo and a small body of British officials acting as advisers to the Egyptian Government under the guidance of Lord Cromer, one of the most splendid and broad-minded administrators that England has ever produced.

Egypt rapidly recovered her financial stability and enjoyed thirty years of material prosperity and of orderly government and justice never before known to her. The construction of huge dams on the Nile extended the area and increased the productivity of Egyptian agriculture. Foreign trade and industry flourished. Egypt became a favorite winter resort for tourists from all countries, and Cairo the center of a cosmopolitan society, usually rather anti-English, in which the French language and French influence predominated. Much more truthfully than when Ismail coined the phrase, Egypt was almost an African corner of Europe. But a new generation at the same time grew up which had never "known Joseph or the days of the oppression" and had forgotten the desolation from which England had rescued it, whilst with the very training which British control brought with it, it was acquiring a new self-respect and a new consciousness of nationhood, with which Lord

Cromer himself advised the British Government to reckon even before he left Egypt in 1907, and which had already induced him, I may remind you, to single out for political advancement the veteran National-ist who is now prime minister of Egypt, Zaghlul Pasha, upon whom just now mainly depends the prospect of a satisfactory settlement of the Egyptian question.

The reaction against British political tutelage and the increasing influence of foreigners of all nationali-ties, not by any means only, nor even chiefly, British, who continued through the default of the Egyptians themselves to control the whole economic life of the country, and in the background the always latent hos-tility of a Mohammedan people to the ascendancy of an infidel power, combined to produce a new and loud-voiced nationalist movement among the West-ern-educated classes which was only temporarily arrested by the outbreak of the Great War.

The first result of the war when Turkey entered into it was to sever Egypt's loosening connection with the Ottoman Empire and to lead to the establish-ment of a British Protectorate. The Khedive Abbas Hilmi had long been notoriously hostile to England, who stood between him and his hankerings after despotic power; and, as he was at Constantinople when the European War first broke out and remained there after Turkey joined the Germanic powers, he was deposed, and a new ruler, Prince Hussein, chosen by England from the reigning dynasty, was installed with the higher title of Sultan of Egypt, but he died prematurely. His ministers stood as loyally as he had by the Allies all through the war, and what-ever may have been the secret sympathies of the

Egyptian masses—who had no love for the Turk, though he is their brother in the faith—internal tranquillity was never once seriously disturbed as long as the war lasted. But no sooner was the armistice signed in November, 1918, than the leaders of the Egyptian Nationalist Party, who had been biding their time, headed by Zaghlul Pasha, whose faith in British promises had been shaken after Lord Cromer's retirement, waited on the British High Commissioner in Cairo and demanded, in the name of the Egyptian people, the immediate recognition of Egypt's complete independence in conformity with the promise of freedom held forth to nations small as well as great by the spokesmen of the Allied Powers, and, above all, with the principle of self-determination laid down by President Wilson. Wholly preoccupied with the peace settlement in Europe, the British ministers ignored these demands even when a tearing and raging propaganda in support of the Zaghlul programme of complete independence carried with it not only the politically-minded classes but the Egyptian masses, who had undoubtedly suffered great hardships in the compulsory levy of labor corps and of onerous supplies of all kinds from their harvest and cattle, from their donkeys even and their camels, for the needs of the British military forces in Palestine and Syria during the later stages of the war. Egyptian ministers, having vainly asked permission to go to London and be heard in person, resigned, and the deportation of Zaghlul and three of his chief followers to Malta merely fired the powder magazine. A popular explosion followed, with a terrible accompaniment of arson and pillage and even murder, and after the active rebellion had been repressed a long period of passive resistance, in which government officials of the chief state departments in Cairo and the law courts and schools and colleges, and even girls' schools and kindergartens, went on strike and paraded the streets shouting, "Down with the Protectorate," "Down with England," compelled the British Government to recognize that it was not enough to have merely released Zaghlul as they had already done on the recommendation of a new High Commissioner, Lord Allenby. A strong Commission of Enquiry belatedly sent out under Lord Milner, one of the members of the Inner War Cabinet in London as well as one of the ablest of Lord Cromer's assistants in the early days of British control, was met by a tumultuous popular boycott and Egyptian ministers suspected of being secretly in touch with the members of the Commission were bombed in the streets of Cairo. Milner soon realized that the prewar forms of British tutelage could never be revived and that the British Protectorate itself, which the Egyptians professed to have accepted only as a temporary war measure, could not possibly be maintained, except under British martial law, which could not be deemed a permanent instrument of government. He realized, also, that no settlement could take place except in consultation with Zaghlul, whom he visited in Paris on his way home and induced to carry on further negotiations with him in London.

The Commission then frankly recommended, as the only means of reconciling British interests and Egyptian aspirations, the creation of a new relationship between the two countries, based on a bilateral treaty of alliance, and the recognition of Egypt as an independent and sovereign state. Lloyd George and Winston Churchill—unfortunately his chief adviser in the matter—turned a deaf ear at first to the Commission's earnest and statesmanlike recommendations, which might then have provided a reasonable way out. But they had to adopt them later on in a modified but less satisfactory form, when fresh disturbance broke out in Egypt and Lord Allenby, High Commissioner, in accord with his most experienced British advisers in Cairo, declared that without a large army, of which the British people were certainly not in a mood to sanction the use, he could not be responsible for the consequence of a policy of mere force. So on February 28, 1922, Mr. Lloyd George, whilst boldly maintaining that British policy in Egypt remained unchanged, made a new "declaration of principles" to the effect that the British Protectorate over Egypt was terminated and Egypt was acknowledged as an independent sovereign state— England reserving only the conclusion "by free discussion and friendly accommodation" of further agreements concerning the security of the communications of the British Empire in Egypt, the defense of Egypt against all foreign aggression and interference, the protection of foreign communities and of minorities in Egypt, and, finally, the Sudan. Those "principles" were all borrowed from the Milner report, with this tremendous difference however, that the latter proposed to have them set forth in a bilateral treaty by which Egypt would have simultaneously contracted binding obligations in regard to the points now remitted by Mr. Lloyd George to future negotiations without in the meantime securing anything in the shape of binding obligations upon Egypt.

Since then Egypt has been recognized by Great Britain as a free and independent sovereign state. King Fuad has assumed the royal title and appointed his own diplomatic representatives abroad, a new Egyptian constitution has been enacted; martial law has ceased; general elections have been held, and Zaghlul, after having been twice deported, has not only returned to Egypt, but is now Prime Minister, with a huge majority behind him in the new parliament. On the other hand, the points reserved by Mr. Lloyd George for future negotiations are no nearer a settlement. A small British force is still stationed in Cairo and Alexandria, Egypt has become if anything a more important base than ever for British military aviation, whilst at the last Imperial Conference the British Dominions laid renewed stress upon the necessity of safeguarding the Empire's line of maritime communications through the Suez Canal, which can only mean the maintenance of some British force, however small, somewhere in Egypt: and Mr. Ramsay MacDonald has recently declared that no British Government can surrender the administration of the Sudan into solely Egyptian hands.

It is on these outstanding points that Zaghlul has been personally invited to negotiate with British Ministers in London; and whilst one may sympathize with some of the demands which he is likely to raise, it is deeply to be regretted that he has apparently resolved to place in the forefront the very worst one of all, namely, the recovery of Egypt's full rights of sovereignty over the Sudan. For on the same principle of self-determination on which the Egyptians

had based their claims to independence, the people of the Sudan have the right to reject Egyptian rule and have emphatically rejected it. Mohammed Ali conquered the Sudan for Egypt a hundred years ago and Egypt so misruled it for over fifty years that the Sudanese responded at once to the call of an able if fanatical leader who, in the early 80's, drove the Egyptians out with great slaughter. The Mahdi, it is true, himself in turn chastised the Sudanese with scorpions, and Kitchener was hailed as a deliverer when, in 1898, he reconquered Khartum, where Gordon had died in 1884, like the great Christian hero that he was, in a vain attempt to stem the desolating tide of Mahdism. Since then, in recognition of Egypt's financial and military contribution, small as it really was, to the reconquest of the Sudan, the Egyptian flag has been flown side by side with the British flag as an emblem of joint sovereignty; but the administration of the country has been wholly in British hands and has restored to the country a marvelous degree of prosperity when one remembers that under the Mahdi's barbarous despotism its population had been reduced in some fifteen years from eight millions to little more than two millions.

From what England has done for the Sudan she has as yet reaped no direct or substantial benefit, but a large amount of British capital has been sunk in the construction of big dams on the White Nile and Blue Nile which will convert the country into one of the great cotton-growing areas of the world. Opinions vary as to the wisdom of some of these schemes and the Egyptians, noting the tall talk there has been about them in financial and other quarters in London, profess to be alarmed lest they curtail the flow of

Nile water available for Egyptian irrigation, which is the very life of Egypt. In this matter, they are entitled to ample guarantees which will certainly not be refused them. But, apart from any special interest that England may have in the Sudan, she cannot consent to hand over the Sudanese to the Egyptians, whom they hate and despise, and who could never enforce their rule on a much more warlike race, much better equipped today than it ever was before for resistance to Egypt.

Even if Zaghlul himself were to prove open to conviction on this and other points—and like many other patriotic Egyptians he professes to recognize the expediency of a friendly accommodation with England, to whose support Egypt must for a long time still alone look for the maintenance of her independence—he has to reckon with the pledges which he has repeatedly given to his own people and with the unyielding spirit which he has himself taught them. On the other hand, other European nations besides England, who have even larger material interests at stake in Egypt, are watching with jealous and perhaps greedy eyes for the opportunity which may arise for one or other of them should an independent Egypt prove as incapable of governing herself on democratic lines as her former rulers proved of governing her on despotic lines. One of the watchwords of the reawakening Orient in Egypt as elsewhere is that it claims freedom to govern itself badly rather than to be governed well by Occidental masters. But Egypt, unlike Turkey, is a halfway house between the Occident and the Orient, and if the Egyptians, released from British control, cannot keep their halfway house in order, one of the greatest

and, take it all in all, one of the most promising
opportunities for a peaceful readjustment of the relations between the Occident and the Orient will be
turned into fresh causes of conflict between them,
pregnant for both with greater dangers than ever
before, now that the Orient can no longer be dealt
with by the Occident in watertight compartments
and has found a strong bond of union in a common
resentment of the white man's claim to racial supremacy.

THE GREAT INDIAN EXPERIMENT

In India the reawakening of the Orient is taking place under conditions differing very widely from those which I have attempted to describe in other Oriental countries. For nowhere else in the Orient has the ascendancy of the Occident been translated as in India into terms of direct and accepted rulership, and if, as I hope to show, it has nowhere been exercised on the whole and despite many shortcomings, in so fine a spirit and with so genuine a desire to raise the peoples of the Orient onto the higher plane of Western civilization, there can be no graver portent for the future relations between the Occident and the Orient than the rising tide of Indian hostility not merely to British rule, but also to the Western civilization for which British rule in India stands.

Without wishing to defend all the methods by which British dominion over India was achieved or all the purposes to which it has been applied, I think it may be claimed that the British people have sought to discharge not unworthily the heavy responsibilities devolving upon them when, through the disintegration of the Mogul Empire in the latter part of the eighteenth century, the Honorable East India Company, originally a mere trading corporation, grew to be the greatest ruling power in a vast Asiatic subcontinent stretching down from the Himalayan Roof of the World to Cape Comorin, only a few degrees north of the equator, with a multitudinous population numbering nearly one-fifth of the whole human race. By a long process of social and political evolution, the British people had made the rule of law prevail at home, and the American War of Independence had just taught them how fatal it was to revert to arbitrary methods of governance in their oversea possessions. Immediately after his decisive victory at Plassey, in 1757, Clive himself warned British ministers that the responsibilities of government and administration over immensely populous and wealthy territories could not be properly discharged through the uncontrolled agency of a great trading corporation, even as exceptionally equipped and constituted as the East India Company; and when that warning was borne out by revelations of corruption and oppression practiced by officers of the Company in the newly acquired provinces of Bengal, the conscience of the British people was so deeply stirred that, within a year of the Treaty of Paris, by which England formally recognized the independence of the United States of America, Pitt was able to pass his great Government of India Act of 1784, which laid down a new and far-reaching principle for the governance of India, *viz.*, the principle of trusteeship. The East India Company, though not yet superseded by the Crown, was charged to apply that principle in all the territories subject to its authority in India, and it was placed henceforth under the regular control of the British Government and Parliament. Dominion over alien races was for the first time recognized to involve a great moral obligation towards them. Their interests, and not those merely of their alien rulers, were to be a principal consideration. Their rulers were to regard themselves as trustees for those over whom they ruled. It is a principle which in our own times has been at least formally accepted by all Western nations who hold dominion over alien races, and it has been consecrated under a new form by the Covenant of the League of Nations. But to Pitt belongs the credit of having been the first to use the word "trust" in this connection.

The East India Company set its house in order and organized great public services which, whatever their human fallibilities, have maintained to the present day the highest standards of integrity and even-handed justice. England began to send out some of her best and ablest sons to serve her in India. British administrators were not concerned merely to estab-lish law and order in the vast territories confided to their care. They began to look forward. Exactly one hundred years ago, in 1824, one of the greatest of them, Sir Thomas Munro, committed himself in a weighty public document to the definition of Eng-land's mission in India as "the training of Indians to govern and protect themselves." It was a far-reach-ing pronouncement, and though Munro was perhaps still somewhat in advance of his times, he set a new ideal before British statesmanship. The first step clearly was to give Indians the same education which had trained the British people to self-government and self-protection. The atmosphere at home was favorable, and under the same liberal impulse that had carried the great Reform Bill of 1832 in England, the famous minute drafted by Macaulay in 1833, whilst he held high legal office in Calcutta, finally committed the British rulers of India to the intro-duction of Western education, by which alone the peoples of India could be taken into partnership with

Western civilization. That this was a generous extension of the idea of trusteeship can hardly be denied, for Macaulay himself fully realized that if the great experiment of which he constituted himself the advocate could be successfully carried through, England's mission in India would be therewith fulfilled—and fulfilled, he rightly maintained, to her imperishable glory—as the peoples of India would then stand in no further need of tutelage, and, having learned how to govern and protect themselves, would justly claim the right to take charge of their own destinies. Such, too, was his confidence in the superiority of our Western civilization that he had no misgivings as to the success of the experiment, and, indeed, predicted that within a few generations there would be nothing but the color of their skins left to mark the difference between Europeans and Indians brought by Western education into full spiritual communion with the Occident.

Nearly a century has passed since then; a century of internal peace in India, only once broken by the short-lived storm of the Indian Mutiny of 1857; a century which has indeed scarcely stirred the ancient village life of India, *i.e.,* of some two-thirds of its people, dependent for their precarious livelihood on the hazards of fierce sunshine and tropical rainfall, but has profoundly modified the aspect and the mentality of the great cities that are the nerve centers of Indian life; a century of steady material progress and relative prosperity in which India has been equipped with all the mechanical appliances of Western science; a century of multiplied facilities of intercourse with the Occident, in which Western knowledge has spread through successive generations to an increasing number of Indians, and a growing familiarity with our English tongue—though still confined to a small section of the population—has created for the first time in Indian history a new and very real bond of national unity in the possession of a common language; a century which has placed India amongst the great industrial and commercial countries of the world; a century which, in recent years at least, has seen the admission of Indians on equal terms to all the public services and even to the highest civil offices of the state, and the feet of India as a nation set in the path of responsible government by the grant of a great constitutional charter under the British Crown. To quote the royal message conveyed by the Duke of Connaught to the new Indian legislatures which he opened three years ago in King George's name: "For years, it may be for generations, patriotic and loyal Indians had dreamed of Swaraj [i.e., self-government] for their motherland. Today you have the beginnings of Swaraj within my empire and the widest scope and ample opportunity for progress to the liberty which my other Dominions enjoy."

I was present at that impressive ceremony. Within the marble halls of the former Mogul Emperors of India there was gathered together a brilliant array of princes and ruling chiefs of the great Native States, some of them almost as large as the minor states of Europe, who have retained under the British Crown their ancient dynastic rights and almost complete autonomy in matters of internal administration throughout more than a third of the total area of the Indian Empire and over populations equaling nearly a quarter of its total population; and, side by side with these representatives of a still largely medieval India, another more significant if less picturesquely attired body, the elected representatives of the Indian people, from the whole of India subject to direct British administration with a population twice as great as that of the United States, the members of the Council of State and of the All-Indian Legislative Assembly, men of all creeds and races and professions, lifted by Western education to new ideals of a common Indian patriotism, charged with new responsibilities and armed with new powers framed on a more democratic model than the Orient has ever yet known. And the ceremony over which the British prince presided at Delhi was itself the closing and most imposing scene in a series of similar ceremonies which had inaugurated provincial legislatures in the capitals of all the major provinces of India, several of which have as large a population as the British Islands. The fine vision which Sir Thomas Munro had had just a hundred years before of England's mission in India as "the training of Indians to govern and protect themselves" seemed at that moment to be drawing very near to fulfillment.

Yet at the very same moment, within a few miles of Delhi, a vastly different scene was being enacted. For Mahatma Gandhi, saint and prophet in the eyes of a great multitude of his people, was denouncing to a mass meeting of enthusiastic Indians not merely British rule but the whole civilization of the Occident and all its works as Satanic. He exhorted them to rebel against every manifestation of that civilization, to refuse any sort of coöperation with Government, to boycott the new Representative Assemblies as a mere Satanic lure, to shun government schools and

law courts and even hospitals as Satanic, and, as beyond everything else Satanic, all the inventions and
appliances of modern mechanical science and every
form of modern industry. The first symbol of India's
regeneration was to be the domestic spinning wheel
for the weaving of homespun cloth to the exclusion of
foreign imported textiles, so that the Indian should
no longer be clothed in the Nessus robe of Occidental
industrialism.

Though Gandhi was not, on the other hand, entirely blind to some of the shortcomings of his own
people and of the social system of Hinduism, and
though he had the courage not only to conduct a vigorous campaign against native liquor-shops but even
to denounce the cruelty of caste laws which treated
millions of human beings as beyond the spiritual
pale and as socially and even physically "untouchable," it is very difficult to interpret his programme
in any practical terms which the Occidental mind can
apprehend. I saw him several times and had one long
and very interesting conversation with him, which
left me more perplexed than ever, for I vainly tried
to obtain from him some picture of what India would
be like under Swaraj as he understood it. He spoke
vaguely of restoring the old Indian village community, with its Panchayats, or Councils of Elders,
in which, he said, justice would be dispensed "in
accordance with the conscience of India," and of
substituting for "ponderous schools and college
buildings of stone and bricks and mortar," as "sti-
fling," according to him, "to the boy's body as modern educational processes are to his soul," simpler
structures "open to God's air and light in which the
learning of their forefathers would make them free

men once more,'' and then, he added, quit of railways and telegraphs and all other instruments and symbols of Western economic bondage, India would return to the pristine felicity of the Vedic ages. All this was to be achieved by spiritual forces, or, as he called it, the soul force of India, and he himself constantly preached non-violence, and always, although rather vainly, did penance in fasting and prayer for the deeds of often savage violence committed by his followers.

Strangest of all, this Hindu prophet and apostle of non-violence was induced to throw his mantle over a purely Mohammedan movement in support of Turkey, engineered by Indian Mohammedans who did little more than lip-worship to his doctrine of non-violence. The leaders of the Indian Khalifate movement belonged to the new school of Mohammedans, who, turning their backs upon the old traditions of their community, had joined hands in the National Congress with the Hindu Extremists for the subversion of British rule. Some of them, and notably the brothers Mohammed and Shau kat Ali, had been in very close contact with the Young Turks before the war, and after the war their hatred of England had quickly seen its opportunity in the resurgence of Turkey. But they could not hope to carry the bulk of their coreligionists with them unless they affixed a religious label to their pro-Turkish campaign. That label was the Khalifate. The Occident, they preached, was banded together to destroy Islam by robbing the Sultan of Turkey of the territorial and temporal power essential to the discharge of his spiritual duties as Khalif. It was an adroit move and singularly successful. A hundred years ago the Indian

Mohammedans knew little about Turkey and cared less. But much had happened since then and the British rulers of India had themselves been the first to magnify Turkey in the eyes of the Indian Mohammedans at the time of the Crimean War and again when Lord Beaconsfield sent an Indian force to Malta in 1878 in anticipation of another war against Russia in defense of Turkey. Then Abdul Hamid's Pan-Islamic propaganda had spread to India, and Italy's seizure of Tripoli in 1911 and the Balkan Wars of 1912-1913 had filled the Mohammedan world with an anxiety which did not leave Indian Mohammedans untouched. All this was for a time almost forgotten during the Great War, but on the general wave of unrest which followed it, the Indian Mohammedans were swept away from their old moorings by the Khalifate agitators, who knew just how to exploit for their own purposes the religious emotionalism of their people.

Gandhi was swept along with them, and without looking closely into the merits of the case, bestowed his blessing on the Khalifate movement—again to quote his own words to me—because it was "a great demonstration of religious faith on the part of his Mohammedan fellow countrymen," beyond which he felt no call to enquire. He of course did not fail to preach to them the duty of non-violence. But he had reckoned without the militant spirit of Islam and the Khalifate movement was responsible for more outbreaks of violence than anything that Gandhi himself did or taught. The savagery of the Mohammedan Moplahs on the Malabar coast in 1921 recalled to the Hindus, who were the chief sufferers, the worst atrocities perpetrated by the early Mohammedan conquerors of India many centuries ago. It was nominally a rising against British rule, but as their Hindu neighbors refused to join, the Moplahs at once turned upon them, slaughtering, plundering, ravishing women and children, or compelling them at the point of the sword to embrace Mohammedanism. The lesson was not lost on the Hindus in other parts of India and many of them were taught to dread a return to the old days of Mohammedan domination if ever India's connection with Britain were finally severed. The relations between the two communities are more strained than ever at the present day, as recent occurrences have shown and notably the Mohammedan anti-Hindu riots last autumn at Saharanpur. Gandhi's dream of Hindu Mohammedan fraternization is further than ever removed from all reality.

An intolerable strain was put upon the forbearance which the Government of India had extended to the Non-Coöperative movement when Gandhi proclaimed a boycott of the Prince of Wales during his visit to India in the winter 1921-1922. Though some violent rioting occurred as soon as he landed in Bombay, the boycott was on the whole a failure, and Gandhi himself admitted that Government was acting entirely within its rights when it at last had him arrested and placed on his trial as a persistent disturber of the public peace. He was condemned to two years' imprisonment, but, having undergone a dangerous operation in the prison hospital, he was released this winter, and, as soon as he had recovered, he revived his former programme, including passive resistance and at some future date a general refusal to pay taxes, and, for the immediate purposes of national exaltation, he dwelt with renewed insistence upon the virtue of the spinning wheel, at which every Indian aspiring to Swaraj should himself work for half an hour at least every day. During his imprisonment, however, other and less unworldly spirits had been fighting to get control of the Non-Coöperation movement. Gandhi has, in fact, been compelled to weaken on several points of his programme during the last session of the Indian National Congress, now little more than a revolutionary rump, and it was only with great difficulty that he prevailed upon it to mitigate the effects of a scandalous incident in one of its provincial branches which had definitely challenged his cherished doctrine of non-violence. A few months ago a young Bengalee student murdered an inoffensive English merchant in Calcutta whom he admitted to have mistaken for a British official. It was a dastardly crime, but the Bengal branch of the Indian National Congress passed a resolution commending the murderer for his patriotic devotion, and passed it with the support of the new Swarajist leader, Mr. Das, who has in effect now set himself up against Gandhi, without, however, so far venturing on any open revolt against such an object of popular veneration as the Mahatma still is.

Gandhi's frail and ascetic figure, crowned in the eyes of his people with a mystic halo of religious sanctity, which places him above caste, is all the more baffling in that he is himself no mere ignorant fanatic.

A Hindu born in the Bombay Presidency of the relatively lowly caste of Bunnias, or traders, he received a Western education and was called to the Bar in London. It was in South Africa, which he chanced to visit professionally soon after he returned to

India, that he for the first time began to entertain doubts of the superiority of Western civilization when he witnessed the disabilities and humiliations to which his Indian fellow countrymen were subjected under the plea of preserving the superiority and purity of the ruling white race. They were nowhere so badly treated as in the Boer Republics, and in its quarrel with President Kruger, the British Government took up the cudgels for the Indians. In the war between Boer and Briton Gandhi did good personal service on the British side with an ambulance body recruited by him from South African Indians, and when the Boers were beaten and Indian grievances still remained unredressed, he continued the struggle, at heavy cost to himself, and with repeatedly diminished hopes of success, at first by methods of constitutional agitation, and at last by preaching and practicing passive resistance. He became a great student of Tolstoy, but he had also studied the Bible and might have been, he once said, converted to Christianity if he had only found more Christians practicing the teachings of Christ. He was still, however, slow to lose faith in British promises. Even in the Great War, his sympathies were altogether with England and his final repudiation of Western civilization occurred only after the dangerous and savage rising in the Punjab in 1919 led to General Dyer's ruthless action at Amritsar on that black day in our Indian annals, of which, as the Duke of Connaught himself said two years later at Delhi, "the shadow has lengthened over the face of India."

I have dwelt at some length on the strange personality of Mahatma Gandhi because, with his high standards of personal conduct and his genuine repudiation of all worldly ambitions, he seems to personify the moral forces of India's ancient civilization, at war on fundamentals with the Occident's conception of civilization ever since the ferment of Western education was imported into India. Hinduism as a religious system has always been singularly elastic and it has known how to include within its capacious fold the gross polytheism and idol worship of the Indian masses as well as the sublime philosophies and the subtle pantheism and even the somber atheism of many schools of Indian thought which regard all the experiences of mortal life as derived from a world of painful illusion that has no more reality than our dreams have. But as a social system Hinduism has preserved a rigidity for which no parallel can be found elsewhere. Its bedrock is the doctrine of caste, according to which every Hindu is born into a watertight compartment of society from which nothing can release him except rebirth in some future phase of existence, whilst its laws govern every incident of his present life, prescribing minutely those whom he may marry, and eat with, and converse with, and the daily ritual which he must perform, and the manner in which he must be buried and his inheritance distributed, now and forever through an endless cycle of birth and death and rebirth out of death *ad infinitum*. At the apex of the caste system stands the Brahminical caste, semidivine in origin, not, indeed, priestly in our sense of the word, but invested with peculiar spiritual privileges. And below it a long gradation of other castes, in a descending scale, reaching down to millions of human beings who are regarded as outside the pale and treated as untouchable, *i.e.,* that social and physical contact with them is deemed to involve religious pollution. Nothing can be in sharper conflict with Occidental individualism or with modern democracy.

Nowadays the spread of Western education and the everyday exigencies of modern life have led to some relaxation of caste laws, but as to marriage and many other supremely vital matters they are still inflexible. I could give you many illustrations from my own personal experience of the unshaken grip in which caste still holds Hindu society, but I prefer to quote a dramatic incident quite recently related by Lord Ronaldshay, since his return from India, where he was Governor of Bengal, one of the most progressive of Indian provinces.

In the summer of 1917 it was persistently rumored in Calcutta that the ghee, or clarified butter, an indispensable article in all Hindu dietary and even in religious ceremonies, was being grossly adulterated with animal fat and other unholy ingredients. Suspicion fastened on the Marwari traders, who form a wealthy and very orthodox Hindu community in Calcutta. An official enquiry was held and the analysis of ghee sold in the Calcutta bazaars disclosed very widespread and gross adulteration. There was great popular indignation and nowhere was it greater than amongst the Brahmans, who, having unwittingly made use of adulterated ghee for ritual purposes, assembled daily in their thousands to go through the bathing ceremonies of purification on the banks of the river. So intense was the excitement that the question filled the columns of the daily press, to the exclusion even of the raging political controversies about the wickedness of a Satanic Government, and an influential and representative deputation of Hindus waited upon the Governor to press for immediate action. Lord Ronaldshay lost no time. A bill was forthwith drafted and passed through all its stages at a single sitting of the Bengal Legislative Assembly three days later. But what was still more effective was the exercise by the Marwaris themselves of the powers which, as they stated, the caste Panchayats, or Councils, have possessed from times immemorial under the unwritten laws of the country for dealing with offenses against society and religion. A Panchayat consisting of three different committees belonging to three different castes, one of them Brahman, was constituted, and dealt with the principal charges and inflicted very heavy fines and long terms of caste excommunication on the chief offenders. This procedure was accepted as satisfactory, the ceremonies of purification were brought to a close and the Brahmans returned to their homes. I will leave the Governor of Bengal, Lord Ronaldshay, to draw the moral in his own words: "Amid the surroundings of a great Western city of the twentieth century was enacted a scene culled from the drama of Indian life two thousand years or more ago. In this incongruous setting was performed an elaborate ritual reaching far back into Vedic times. The admittedly efficient administrative machinery imported from the West fell into the background of men's minds. It might be called in to assist in guarding against similar trouble in the future, but it was powerless to deal with the situation which had actually arisen. It was to the caste Panchayat, with its laws and its authority rooted in antiquity, that the Indian turned in this emergency which had arisen in

matters affecting the most intimate aspects of his
life.''

Such is the enduring power of customs and traditions inherited from before the dawn of history by
more than two hundred millions of the population of
India who are Hindus, and they still have no slight
hold even on the seventy millions who are Mohammedans, for their forebears were for the most part
Hindus compulsorily converted to Islam during the
long centuries of Mohammedan domination which
preceded British rule. Indian Mohammedans have
not forgotten that the sword of Islam once ruled over
India, and though Islamic monotheism divides them
from their idol-worshiping fellow countrymen, Western civilization is no less repugnant to them as a
civilization deriving from the infidel nations of
Europe, and they are still bitterly aware that it was
British power that dealt the final blow to their own
domination.

In both cases Western education, though carefully
divorced by Government from all denominational
teaching, tended inevitably to undermine the founda-
tions of ancient belief, whether Hindu or Mohammedan, whilst it supplied no new and direct religious
or even moral sanctions to take the place of the older
ones which it often destroyed. It inspired new social
and religious reform movements, which tended to
the subversion of the old order of things even in the
domain of Hindu family life. It threatened also many
vested interests, and above all, in the domain of
Hinduism, those of the higher, and especially of the
Brahminical castes, at a time when political changes
were still in progress which were deeply resented by
other adherents of the old order who often repre-

sented the worst survivals of indigenous administration. Nor was it possible to expound the speeches of Burke and Fox, or to make a textbook of Mill on liberty, or to glorify the love of freedom, which had moulded British institutions and shaped the growth of nationalism on the European continent, to a highly intelligent and imaginative race without inoculating it with the germs of Western freedom of thought in the sphere of politics as well as of religion.

But Englishmen saw no reason at first to distrust the results of Western education. Young Indians flocked to the schools and colleges which government or missionary enterprise multiplied in response to the growing demand of Indian parents in all the chief cities of India. Progress was only temporarily checked by the great Mutiny of 1857, though behind the military revolt in which Mohammedan troops took the lead, there was a barely concealed explosion of all the reactionary forces of Hinduism as well as of Islam. In fulfillment of pre-Mutiny promises the first Indian University was founded in 1859 at Calcutta, and others were soon opened in several of the great cities for the purpose of raising Western education to a still higher level. Another generation grew up, however, that began not unreasonably to claim with great urgency a larger share in the government and administration of the country, as the legitimate reward of educational fitness. But the Mutiny had given a lamentable setback to the Englishman's faith in the loyalty of Indians, and standards of efficiency which few Indians could yet be expected to satisfy were set up as the supreme cult of a great and highly centralized bureaucracy, which was, curiously enough, less closely controlled by the

British Parliament, as soon as, after the Mutiny, the East Indian Company had been wound up and India had passed under the direct sovereignty of the Crown. Even social relations between the two races had lost a good deal of their pre-Mutiny cordiality, and the gradual estrangement of the Western educated classes from the Anglo-Indian bureaucracy was reflected in the rapid growth of the Indian press which used and abused the freedom it enjoyed to attack, often with little regard to decency or to truth, every policy of the Government of India and every action of government servants.

A momentous parting of the ways occurred after the heated racial controversies over the famous Ilbert Bill, when a small group of progressive Indians, most of them still quite thoroughly devoted to the British connection, founded the Indian National Congress in 1884 as an informal parliament to ventilate Indian grievances on constitutional lines, and to appeal also to public opinion in England over the heads of the Anglo-Indian bureaucracy. Had it been given a helping and guiding hand at the outset, it might have fulfilled a useful purpose, though there was something in the official argument that it represented only the Hindus and not the Mohammedans, who at first held entirely aloof from it, and amongst the Hindus themselves only the new urban middle classes, and was much less closely in touch than the British District officers with the wishes and needs of the vast agricultural population. But the growing racial pride of the Indians stiffened the Englishman's own racial stubbornness, and the Congress, cold-shouldered and often treated with almost open derision, drifted into an attitude of systematic and often unreasoning opposition, and the social reform movement, to which it was originally pledged, gave way to a purely political reform movement on which it was much easier for Indians of all castes to combine against an alien Government. The fact, too, that for the first time a single political organization, however loose, drew Indians together from all parts of India, lent more reality to the new sense of common nationhood and afforded a new opportunity of giving expression to it, though English was the one common language which the Indian National Congress could use for denouncing British rule as the denial of Indian nationhood.

Whilst British rulers were still slow to respond, and only grudgingly, to the political demands even of the most moderate and sober Indian public opinion as formulated by the Western educated classes, the emergence of Japan and her resounding victories in Manchuria over a great European power shook the Indian belief in the material invincibility of the Occident. To the reactionary forces of Indian society still banded together against all the liberal influences of Western education were added, during the same first decade of the twentieth century, new revolutionary forces drawing their inspiration from the apostles of revolution in the Occident, and notably in Russia, where secret conspiracies and political assassinations seemed to be the only effective means of achieving social and religious freedom.

A traditional aversion to all forms of manual labor as degrading to their caste had driven large numbers of young Indians to struggle, at excessive cost to themselves and their parents, through long years of school and college life for which they were quite unfitted, and the end of it all was too often the bitterness of failure in their examinations and the consequent closing against them of the avenues to lucrative employment, and especially to official employment by the state, which they had come to regard as the proper reward of even a "failed" B.A. Such misfits were apt to degenerate into a sort of intellectual proletariat, amongst whom a propaganda of "direct action" found many willing recruits, when more astute wire-pullers in the background assured them that the call to action proceeded from the motherland's avenging deities. Morbidly emotional youths took solemn vows to the terrific Goddess Kali, the consort of Shiva, himself the God of Destruction, to sacrifice "white goats" in her honor, meaning English officials; and not only English officials, but Indians whose only crime was to be loyal servants of Government fell victims to youthful fanatics, whose crimes the more violent organs of Indian public opinion scarcely hesitated to glorify, or at least to palliate, as the expression of an heroic if misguided patriotism. Even Indians who were alarmed at the demoralization which such crimes revealed amongst the rising generation imputed a large share of responsibility to the tardiness and inadequacy of the concessions with which Government had hitherto met India's legitimate aspirations towards political freedom. They were not satisfied with municipal institutions kept in official leading strings or with the small Legislative Councils which gave to Indian members little more than a consultative voice in public affairs or with the subordinate position which all but a few Indians held in the public service. The Government of India demanded and obtained from London full authority to take such repressive measures as were needed to deal with political outrages, but British public opinion was perplexed and alarmed, and, with the advent of a Liberal Government and John Morley's appointment to the India Office, a serious attempt was made to meet Indian desires. The Indian Councils Act of 1909 gave a large extension of powers to both the central and provincial legislatures, and Indians were for the first time appointed to the Viceroy's Executive Council, hitherto the citadel of British authority in India, and to the India Council in London, also until then a stronghold of the Anglo-Indian bureaucracy. These measures were at first warmly welcomed in India, and when at the end of 1911 King George and his Consort paid their first visit to India as reigning sovereigns they were greeted with universal enthusiasm, carried in some places to the embarrassing length of the semidivine worship which Hindu tradition accords to kingship. But India is always liable to be swept by great waves of emotion, which often subside as rapidly, and the new revolutionary forces were shown to be still in being when just a year afterwards a bomb was thrown, with very nearly mortal effect, at the Viceroy, Lord Hardinge, whilst he was making his state entry into Delhi, which the King-Emperor in person had proclaimed to be the new capital of his Indian Empire, as a more central and historic city than Calcutta.

Political agitation had become once more acute when the Great War broke out. Then it was suddenly hushed, and England herself was astonished at India's wonderful outburst of loyalty. Princes and people were proud to see the Indian army sent to

Europe to fight shoulder to shoulder with the British
army in France, and right gallantly did it help to
hold up the German invasion during the very critical
winter of 1914-1915. Mr. Asquith, who was then
Prime Minister, gave expression to England's grati-
tude when he declared that Indian questions would
henceforth have to be approached from "a new angle
of vision." But in the protracted stress of war, the
fulfillment of that promise was so long delayed that
all the old discontents flamed up afresh in the shape
of another raging and tearing campaign, this time
for immediate Home Rule. British Ministers were at
last compelled by urgent appeals from the Government of India itself to lay aside their war maps for
a moment, and remember Mr. Asquith's pledges.

In August, 1917, Mr. Montagu, an advanced Radical who had lately gone to the India Office, made the
most momentous declaration on Indian affairs to
which the British Parliament had listened since the
days of Pitt. "The purpose of British policy in
India" was, he stated, "not only the increasing association of Indians in every branch of the administration, but also the greatest development of self-governing institutions with a view to the progressive
realization of responsible government in India as an
integral part of the British Empire." He himself
proceeded shortly afterwards to India, and drew up,
in consultation not only with the then new Viceroy,
Lord Chelmsford, but with representative Indians
of all political complexions, an exhaustive report
which served as a basis for the great Government of
India Bill adopted by both houses of Parliament at
the end of 1919.

The principal feature of this new Constitutional

Charter is the creation of representative assemblies for all India and for each of the provinces elected on the widest franchise possible in the present stage of Indian social evolution. Whilst the ultimate powers of the Central Government responsible to British Parliament have been fully safeguarded, Indians henceforth formed almost one-half of the Viceroy's Executive Council, or Cabinet. In the provinces the new system of Diarchy was introduced, which divided the provincial government into two wings, consisting respectively of the Governor's Executive Council and of Indian Ministers, the latter responsible to the provincial legislature in the fields of administration specially delegated to them, such as education, sanitation, public works, and other subjects, now known as the "transferred" subjects, with which the bulk of the population is most closely concerned. The Act further contemplated an extension of the fields immediately handed over to administration by Indian Ministers, to take place after successive periods of ten years, according to the measure of success achieved by them, until they should cover the whole range of provincial administration, when the same processes were to be applied to All-Indian administration reserved for the present to the Central Government. When provincial autonomy should have gradually expanded into All-Indian autonomy, India would enjoy the same rights of self-government as the other self-governing Dominions in the British Commonwealth of Nations. To facilitate decentralization, definite sources of revenue were at the same time assigned to the provinces for purely provincial purposes, whilst they had in return to make regular annual contributions from their revenues to the All-

Indian Exchequer. The Indianization of the public services was to proceed on parallel lines.

Received at first with general satisfaction by the Moderate Nationalists as a substantial stride towards a complete self-government, many of the older Anglo-Indian officials did not conceal their dislike of such a transfer of the powers hitherto reserved to them, which they had wielded not only with undisputed authority, but, they contended, with a fuller knowledge of the needs of the masses than the Western-educated Indians possessed, and also perhaps with a fuller sense of responsibility. The Extreme Swarajists, on the other hand, at once poured a stream of abuse upon the whole scheme of reforms as wholly inadequate, if not as a perfidious attempt to force India into the framework of Occidental institutions in order finally to destroy her own inherited civilization, and they agitated more vehemently than ever for immediate and full *Swaraj*, by which most of them meant nothing less than complete independence.

It was just about this time too that labor unrest, an entirely novel feature in Indian life, began to assume a dangerous aspect in a widespread epidemic of lightning strikes, frequently accompanied by violent riots. Gandhi may denounce industrialism and commercialism as amongst the most Satanic gifts of the Occident, but they have come to India to stay, and the first use which the All-Indian Legislature has made of the fiscal freedom granted to India under its new constitutional charter has been to raise the tariffs on imports, and especially on British imports, for the better protection of her own industries—and this with the coöperation even of many of Gandhi's followers! Higher wages and the attractions of town life have for the last twenty or thirty years been steadily tempting away from their villages into the urban centers of modern Indian industry hundreds of thousands of unskilled workers, almost wholly illiterate and densely ignorant, with no capacity to organize themselves. Labor legislation, too long delayed, has only recently mitigated the harsh conditions under which they worked in their factories and lived in the terribly congested slums into which they and their families were packed. Indian employers, with no traditions behind them, were slow to acquire the sense of duty to their men which European employers have for the most part brought with them to India. Trade Unions have sprung up like mushrooms, but they are largely the creation of professional agitators, who, if they have no direct contact with Moscow, might well have graduated in the school of Russian Bolshevism, which has gripped, it must be remembered, the whole of Central Asia down to the borderlands of India, and claims to have trained a special class of revolutionary missionaries for its propaganda in India itself.

A period of intense financial stringency, partly due to the heavy burden of military expenditure and partly to severe economic depression, itself a backwash from Europe, successive bad harvests, two frightful epidemics of influenza which within eight months swept away eight millions of people and lowered the vitality of many more millions, combined to produce innumerable streams of discontent even amongst the rural population, which all went to swell the broad tide of Non-Coöperation, whilst the aftermath of the Punjab troubles and the Khalifate move-

ment was there to provide always a common de-nominator of racial hatred.

Out of this poisoned atmosphere the reforms had to battle their way during the first three years of the new Indian legislatures, and on the whole with no small measure of success. The All-Indian Legislative Assembly, under the able guidance of Sir Frederick Whyte, whose parliamentary experience at West-minster carried great weight with the Indian mem-bers, displayed on many critical occasions remark-able wisdom and restraint. Personal relations, often of the friendliest character, grew up between Indians and Englishmen, official and non-official. The Indian Moderates, who were in a large majority, as the Extreme Swarajists, had shut themselves out of the legislatures in obedience to Gandhi's injunctions, were only driven into unyielding opposition when, a few months before the new general elections, Gov-ernment, very inopportunely, and, as many think, quite unnecessarily, insisted on increasing the salt duties in order to balance an otherwise not unreason-able budget. The Viceroy, Lord Reading, straining perhaps unduly the powers reserved to the Govern-ment of India under the new Constitution, finally carried the salt duties over the head of the Assembly by the procedure known as "certification," and the Moderate party had to go to the polls at the general elections held this winter heavily handicapped by their failure to prevent the enactment of a tradi-tionally most unpopular fiscal measure. Many of their best men were defeated by the Extremists, who on this occasion declined to boycott the elections as they had done three years ago. But the Extremists are not yet in a majority, and, split up into several factions now that they are inside the legislatures, they find it less easy or are less disposed to persevere in the wrecking policy which was declared to be their purpose and their excuse for entering them. They still, of course, carry on a vigorous propaganda throughout the country for immediate and full *Swaraj*, and the Moderates have been dragged so far in their wake as to press for the appointment by the British Government of a Commission of Enquiry with a view to the speedy enlargement of the present reforms, without waiting for the appointed period of ten years from the date of the Government of India Act of 1919. To this demand the Labor Government at home has not seen its way to accede, though some of its members had made many rash, if vague, promises before they expected to have to assume the responsibilities of Government. Mr. Ramsay Mac-Donald, with whom I had the honor of serving on a Royal Commission which spent two winters in India before the Great War on an enquiry into the Indian Public Services, has enough personal knowledge of India to share the misgivings of most Englishmen who know the country as to the wisdom of relaxing any further at this juncture the diminished powers of government and administration which India's new Constitution, not yet quite five years old, has reserved for British agencies of control.

England has her duty to perform towards the politically-minded classes whose aspirations towards a larger measure of self-government, or even independence, she has encouraged, and, one might almost say, created, by the diffusion of Western education in India. But she has also her duty to perform towards the countless millions whom the breath of Occidental civilization has scarcely yet touched. There are multitudes of Indians who toil and moil in remote rural districts who never see a white man's face, and the vast majority still put their trust in British rule as the one that divides them least and offers them the best chance of fair and equal treatment, free from all the class and race and caste prejudices of which Indians can very rarely completely divest themselves. England has equally to discharge her duty towards the rulers of the native states, who rely upon ancient treaties with her for the preservation of their autonomous rights against revolutionary changes in the rest of India. Nor can England forget that she is responsible for the great economic interests bound up with the maintenance of internal peace and with the security against foreign aggression which a severance of her connection with India would jeopardize to the detriment, and perhaps the ruin, of all concerned. India has always been and is still so largely dependent upon the energies of Government in many fields which are left in Occidental countries to the initiative of private enterprise, that there is an exceptional need in the public services for expert knowledge which Indians are not yet in a position to supply. The Indianization of the services is proceeding rapidly, but the pace cannot be forced merely to satisfy Indian impatience, at the risk of a complete breakdown of the delicate and complex machinery set up by practical experience and trained intelligence in the course of many generations. No British Prime Minister could therefore venture to take any step that might spell abrupt abdication. Nor is there as yet, I believe, any reason to despair of a happy ending to a period of administrative as well as con-

stitutional transition, because it has proved more
stormy than a perhaps excessive optimism anticipated.

The situation may still be far from reassuring,
but the acute phase of Non-Coöperation seems to
have passed away, the Khalifate movement has been
scotched, if not killed, by the Turkish abolition of the
Khalifate, and the racial passions which they had
unloosed might have subsided even more rapidly had
they not been roused afresh by the deplorable racial
issues constantly arising out of the treatment of
Indians in South Africa and more recently still in
Kenya. In South Africa British Ministers could at
any rate plead that it was not within their power to
interfere with the domestic legislation of a self-
governing dominion, but no such plea could avail in
the case of Kenya, a Crown Colony under the direct
control of the Colonial Office in London. Even the
remonstrances of the Government of India, though
it pleaded with great vigor as the spokesman of all
political parties and voiced the sentiment of the
whole of India, were powerless to arrest, or even ap-
preciably to mitigate, the anti-Indian policy imposed
on the Colonial Office by the white settlers in Kenya,
whose leaders openly threatened to use violence if
they were thwarted. Yet only less than two years
previously, the Imperial Conference in London, with
General Smuts alone dissenting on behalf of South
Africa, had pledged itself on principle to equality of
treatment for Indians throughout the Empire!

To conclude, the Orient and the Occident are being
drawn more and more closely together by all the
mechanical appliances of Western civilization. Tele-

graph and wireless, fast steamers and railways and
motors are annihilating distance and time. Out-
wardly, the chief cities of the Orient, and especially
in India, have adopted, or are adopting, most of the
material equipment of the Occident. Intellectually
and politically the Occident reacts with increasing
rapidity upon the Orient. Whilst the masses have
scarcely been stirred by the breath of the Occident, a
more or less highly educated class has grown up, and
can read and write and speak English, sometimes
quite admirably. The best of Indian brains are as
acute as the best Western brains. There are Indian
judges and lawyers, doctors and engineers, men of
letters and men of science, poets and artists, writers
and political leaders, quite capable of competing in
their own field with the men of the Occident who were
once their teachers. Textbooks in schools and colleges have been for the most part borrowed from the
Occident but there are signs everywhere of an indigenous literary and artistic revival, and, if it is to
Occidental research that the Orient owes its much
larger knowledge today of even its own past history,
there are Indians now doing admirable work in the
same field. Many have been brought up almost exclusively on Occidental literature, of which, at first
at any rate, they preferred the best. Today, unfortunately, the public bookstalls of the Orient are
littered with a great deal of Occidental trash, often
in cheap vernacular translations, just as the cinemas
generally parade the worst possible pictures of Occidental life. With increased facilities of travel, many
more Indians come to England for purposes of study
or business or pleasure, and often see only the seamy
sides of our civilization, whilst there go out to India

many Englishmen of a class less desirable than that with which Indians were formerly familiar, who from ignorance or carelessness often grossly offend Indian susceptibilities, and having no other superiority to boast of, drag the coattails of racial superiority. The influence of the press, itself an entirely modern production imported from the Occident, has become enormous. Many of the Indian newspapers, owned, edited, and financed by Indians, are written and published in English, even when they are most bitterly anti-English in spirit and tone, and they give the cue to innumerable vernacular newspapers far more crude and violent. Under the stimulus of the Occident, the Orient has learned to develop its immense natural resources, and its markets, more and more closely linked up in trade, industry, and finance with those of the Occident, respond automatically to every wave of prosperity and depression that beats upon them from London or Paris or New York. The majority of the great cotton mills of Bombay and Nagpur have passed under Indian control, and the railways, without which the British armies could never have fought the Syrian or Mesopotamian campaigns during the Great War, were laid with Indian rails from the Tata Iron and Steel Works in Bengal, as splendidly equipped as any in Yorkshire.

Western education has been for the Orient the tree of knowledge of good and evil. Whether the good shall prevail over the evil constitutes the supreme test to which the civilization of the Occident as a whole is being subjected today throughout the Orient. It is not merely or mainly the political ascendancy of any one Western power over these or those peoples of the Orient that is at stake. It is not merely or mainly whether President Wilson's formula of self-determination is, or was intended to be, applicable to the nations of the Orient, whose independence might very well mean a reversion to Oriental forms of national and social life entirely incompatible with any fruitful intercourse with the Occident. The real issue, in India at least, and it will, I think, be decisive for other parts of the Orient, is whether the Orient can be brought to adopt the democratic type of human society which the most progressive nations of the Occident have slowly evolved as affording the largest opportunities for individual and collective freedom combined with the restraining sense of individual and collective responsibility. Almost the only forms of government which the Orient has ever known have been theocracy and autocracy with alternating periods of license and anarchy, and none of these has favored the development of character, which is what the Orient chiefly lacks.

Hence the importance of that great British experiment in India which has now reached its most critical stage. There are only 150,000 Englishmen, including the British garrisons, in the whole of India, scattered amongst a vast population of over three hundred millions. It is less than ever by the sword that England can hope to rule India, and there is less desire than ever amongst the British people to hold alien races under their subjection by the sword. What is to be feared at present is not a sudden upheaval against British rule, but a steady estrangement of the best elements in India itself, without whose co-operation the whole scheme of reforms may languish and perhaps perish before it has ever been given a fair trial. Then with the steady attrition of British power, the weight of India might ultimately be thrown by the growth of racial hatred wholly and irrevocably into the scales against any enduring peace between the Occident and the Orient. By her geographical position, by her great natural resources, by the splendid intellectual capacity of many of her people, by the fighting qualities of her martial races, and by the political endurance of her vast population, she is bound to wield a decisive influence on the issue which is now pending throughout the Orient.

It will be an evil day for the Occident if all the other political, social, and economic problems with which it is faced in the Orient come to be merged into one comprehensive color problem which must irresistibly unite against the Occident all the different races and creeds which still divide the Orient. In America you have that color problem in one of its acutest forms within your own borders. You have it at your gates in the shape of Asiatic immigration. Further afield you have it in the Philippines. We are face to face with it in many parts of the Orient, and it lurks behind all our troubles in India. Its solution threatens to become the acid test of our Occidental civilization, which is yours as well as ours, and even, I will venture to add, of our common Christianity, which is, I firmly believe, in its broadest sense, the one sure foundation of our common civilization. I cannot for that very reason bring myself to imagine that no solution can be found to it in spite of the tremendous difficulties with which it bristles on all sides, and it is in the hope of stimulating an earnest desire to ensure its solution that I have laid so much stress on the ominous part it is playing and, until it is solved, will go on playing in the relations between the Occident and the reawakening Orient.

I. THE LIBERAL MOVEMENT IN JAPAN

II. THE ORIGIN AND GROWTH OF THE LA-
BOR MOVEMENT IN JAPAN

BY YUSUKE TSURUMI

I

THE LIBERAL MOVEMENT IN JAPAN

In this chapter, I propose to show how in spite of the imperialist turn in affairs which followed the Restoration, liberal forces continued to furnish a fermenting leaven to national life. I also intend to explain how the constitutional machine established in 1889 operated in such a way as to hold down to the lowest degree the pressure of the rising liberal influences. This is a vital point in the argument and I deem it necessary to elaborate it in great detail. Finally, I propose to show how the economic revolution which followed the outbreak of the World War in 1914 created for the first time in Japan a large, independent, and prosperous middle class to form the basis of a substantial liberal movement. Then I intend to explain how democratic, not to say radical, ideas made rapid progress in Japan, partly under the influence of President Wilson's lofty idealism and later as a result of the overthrow of autocratic systems in Europe. This middle class, backed by the rising labor movement, was making a steady advance upon the conservative party, in spite of the limited suffrage and the strategic position of the bureaucracy, when like a bolt from the blue sky came the Immigration Bill of 1924, bringing in its train grave consequences for the future of Japan. Such in outline is the substance of this chapter.

I

In accordance with this plan, I shall first sketch

briefly the conflict of liberal and conservative forces which followed the Restoration.

It was the soldiers of four great clans that had overthrown the Shogunate. They were Satsuma, Choshu, Tosa, and Hizen. These conservative elements, though supreme in the Government, were unable to keep their ranks long intact. The Tosa clan, headed by Itagaki, was the first to become estranged, because in Itagaki ran a radical vein; he was the first to advocate representation of the people. He left the Government and his banner became a rallying point for the forces of democracy. His followers, imbued with the French Radicalism of the Rousseau school, demanded equality and liberty. The group he organized became the Liberal Party of Japan and later served as the foundation for the present Seiyukai and Seiyuhonto, decidedly conservative parties. Among Itagaki's followers were some who subscribed to republican principles, and even so great a scholar as the late Baron Hiroyuki Kato, who died a staunch conservative, wrote in 1874, in his *New Theory of the State,* that of all systems of government the republican was the best. Other young men went further than this and were quite radical in their views. I might add that later Baron Kato, when he was made a privy councilor, had a hard time to buy up all the old copies of this book.

One interesting instance is that of Yurei Mori, who later became Minister of Education and laid the foundation of Japan's educational system; he advocated the scrapping of the Japanese language and the adoption of English instead as our national tongue. His contention was that the energy of the nation was exhausted by the foolish memorizing of the Chinese characters, running from ten to fifty thousand in number.

Even if the late Viscount Mori's suggestion had been adopted and carried out in Japan, I secretly wonder whether the English in use in Japan would have been the same as that used in this country. The English language was much ameliorated by crossing the Atlantic Ocean, and there is no reason why it should not be even more improved by crossing a still larger ocean, the Pacific. I think I can illustrate this by a story. Before the earthquake there was in the city of Yokohama a Japanese tailor whose specialty was to make fur coats for foreign ladies. He started to put up a huge signboard on the top of his roof, much larger than his own house, on which he wrote in remarkable English as follows: "We make overcoats either with your skin or ours."

The Hizen clan, having no strong army, could not hold out against Satsuma and Chosu, and was forced to leave the seat of power. It followed Tosa into the ranks of the opposition. The world-famous Okuma, the Hizen leader, dramatically tendered his resignation from the Government on the issue of the Constitution's promulgation in 1881. Many able young men left the Government with him and he organized the Progressive Party, along more or less English political ideas. Okuma's Progressive Party, minus many of its progressive elements, is the Kenseikai, which is in power now.

With Tosa and Hizen removed from the inner circle of power, the Satsuma and Choshu clans now entered upon a period of supremacy which was to last about forty years. Cleverly stealing the thunder of their political opponents, they promulgated a con-

stitution of their own. How Prince Ito of Choshu was
selected to draft a constitution, how he was converted
to the theories of Lorenz von Stein and returned
from abroad to write a constitution modeled after
the German style is a story too well known to be
repeated here.

While the conservative forces were striving by
every means to strengthen and consolidate their position, the fight for democracy was being waged in the
fields of journalism and education.

Japan's samurai, proud fighting men of pre-Res-
toration days, found themselves in difficult straits
in the new society. Instead of the incomes they had
received previously in the form of rice, they received
in a lump sum from the Government national bonds
with which they were to begin new lives. Most of
them, because they had no business training, lost
most of their bonds in commercial ventures and the
big business men and landlords profited at their ex-
pense. In the discontented frame of mind which
such conditions might be expected to produce, these
former samurai became the most enthusiastic members of the newly formed political parties, entered in
large numbers the professions of journalism and
teaching, and began with new vigor to lay the foundation for a democratic movement. And they were
destined to become the nucleus of the solid middle
class of Japan.

Most of the famous writers of the early days of
Meiji were samurai who before the Restoration had
been in the service of the Tokugawas. Their literary
weapons naturally were used in frequent attacks on
the Government. Many of their fellows were active
in educational work, one of the most distinguished

being Yukichi Fukuzawa, the founder of the famous
Keio University. This noted educator, the man responsible for the introduction of English utilitarian-
ism in Japan, preached a doctrine of individual self-
respect and independence. Fukuzawa's influence on
national thought is plainly to be seen even now.
Through his gate passed men like Inukai, Ozaki, and
Sanji Muto, all prominent and vigorous advocates
of progressivism in the present House of Representatives.

Okuma also started a university of his own, which
is now known as Waseda University. This institution
was to supply most of Japan's journalists, while
Keio's graduates for the most part went into business. Great numbers of students sent out from these
universities strengthened the forces of progressivism for the coming test of strength with the conservatives.

The Government was not slow in counteracting
the educational and journalistic activities of the opposition. It organized a strong and thorough system
of education. To my mind, the major part of Japan's
success is due to her educational system. I think that
the amount of illiteracy is now below 5 per cent.
Unlike your country, Japan gives a leadership to the
government schools all out of proportion to that
assigned to private institutions. A strict examina-
tion system was adopted. Students who stood well in
the examinations of the higher government schools
were given a kind of recognition by the state. This
was particularly the case with the graduates of the
Imperial Universities, which were at the apex of the
whole educational system. If you go through the list
of prominent Japanese, say under sixty years of age,

you will find that they were in most cases formerly students who stood high in the Imperial Universities. Take the present cabinet, for example; eight out of eleven members are graduates of the government schools, and six of these, including the Premier, are graduates of the Imperial University of Tokyo, mostly head boys.

In this way the government schools attracted the major portion of the talent of the country. Into the minds of the students was instilled a strong sense of conservative nationalism. Most of the graduates of the Imperial Universities went into the civil service, where they could find the best chance of promotion based on the merit system. Thus Satsuma and Choshu strengthened their position by incorporating within their ranks a large part of the finest brains of the country. As the young men thus drawn from the universities were mostly of the middle class—in some cases from the labor classes—the conservatives thus skimmed the cream of the ambitious elements that might have given them serious trouble otherwise. This was the secret of the endurance of their power through such a long lapse of time. This helps to explain also the preponderance of the executive against the representative branch of the Government.

Out of the conflict of the liberal and conservative forces came many exciting contests previous to the adoption of the Constitution in 1889. The opposition often carried on violent agitation. Accordingly the Government grew more ruthless in its efforts to suppress the rising tide of democracy. The Constitution drafted by Ito was on the whole a very conservative instrument, but still it was considered radical by many conservatives of the day.

The conservative elements found their strongest and ablest exponent in Yamagata, a Choshu man who later became a field marshal and prince. The country's political history during the greater part of the Meiji Era centered around an unending fight between Ito and Yamagata, fellow clansmen. Although Ito enjoyed greater popular favor than his rival, Yamagata's invisible power was stronger in every department of the Government.

Yamagata created the strong army which won Japan's two foreign wars, achievements which added enormously to his prestige. He then proceeded carefully to strengthen his influence in the House of Peers, which he utilized to bolster up the bureaucracy. His third line of defense was the Privy Council, where eventually he sent most of his trusted followers.

The Japanese Parliament was first organized in 1890, but it was preceded by another important reform—the creation of prefectural assemblies in 1878. While Ito was bent on setting up a national parliament, Yamagata was busy with a programme for granting local autonomy which he contended should precede the establishment of a national House of Representatives.

The people enfranchised by the law establishing local assemblies were middle-class landlords, so the agrarian middle class received its political emancipation before the corresponding class in urban centers. It was not surprising that these provincial landlords, with their new privileges, were destined to become an important factor in Japanese politics.

Gradually they discovered that the policy of the central Government favored the great commercial interests of the cities—a discovery which was followed by the transference of their political allegiance to the parties of Itagaki and Okuma. The main strength of Japanese political parties, then as now, lay in the agrarian districts; and this circumstance gave certain peculiar features to the Japanese labor movement, which will be discussed later.

It was in the House of Representatives that the conservative forces of Yamagata clashed with those of democracy. First Itagaki, then Okuma, and later Ito himself led the opposition. Every variety of political combination was resorted to in the attempt to curb the power of the conservatives, but to trace these maneuvers and deal with personalities of the period would require too much space. As my object is to deal with the present, the important point is the result; it is sufficient to say that, despite the fact that Yamagata was all-powerful, the House of Representatives kept on increasing its power until it is impossible now to ignore it in organizing a cabinet. General elections were fought out very severely. The conservatives were far from being scrupulous and resorted to means not altogether laudable. They employed the tactics of corruption and police intervention.

The Government has always been in a strong position to use these two weapons, and the result has been the constant victory of the government party, with the single exception of this year's election. Here we can again discern the economic forces working behind it. The Government has always been supporting and has always been supported by big business, and has found it easy to get campaign expenses, whereas the party or parties in opposition have found it very difficult to summon necessary financial support.

II

Now I come to the second part of my outline, namely, an explanation of the way in which the constitutional machine established in 1889 has operated to hold down the pressure of liberal forces.

First of all, of course, is the limited suffrage, which gives Japan an electorate of about three million voters, notwithstanding the recent extension of the franchise. The great mass of laborers and members of the lower middle class are deprived of the ballot altogether.

Even with this handicap, the politics of Japan would have been far more liberal had it not been for the enormous expenses involved in parliamentary elections. In explaining Japanese politics we arrive at this or start from this. The cost of elections presents one of the most perplexing problems confronting Japan today, and it is necessary for me to lay considerable emphasis on this part of my subject.

When voting was introduced it was a great novelty and few people knew anything about Western election methods. In the first campaign of 1890, election expenses were almost nothing. For example, the noted scholar Nishi was returned from the city of Okayama with the entire outlay of one yen, or fifty cents in American money. This was the amount he spent for his transportation in a rickshaw from his village to Okayama. But according to a conservative estimate for the election of last May, candidates spent on the average 50,000 yen. The maximum is

said to have been 400,000 yen. Cases of 200,000 yen
are not very rare. The minimum record is that of Mr.
Inukai, the leader of the Kakushin Club or Reform
Club, who has been returned unopposed since the
opening of the Diet. He makes no campaign; he just
sends letters of thanks to every voter after election;
this costs him something like one thousand yen.

This extraordinary cost of elections is the curse
of Japanese politics and some of our greatest political evils are traced to this one outstanding cause. By
concentrating our attention on this single fact, we can
understand the real political situation of present-day
Japan very clearly.

Let us study the effects this has brought in its
train.

1. In the first place, the necessity of great outlays
has had a decisive influence on the character of candidates for Parliament. It has practically shut the
door of the House to the middle class and also to the
laboring people. Independent men who do not care
to give pledges to their rich friends have found it
impossible to get into political life. Some have man-
aged somehow to raise expenses for one or two elections, but could not last long. There are cases of
downright tragedy; the master of many a well-to-do
family has gone into politics with sincere, patriotic
motives and ruined not only his own career, but also
the life of his whole family. To run for a seat in the
House sends cold shudders through the hearts of the
candidate's family and friends in Japan.

2. In the second place, the high cost of elections
naturally means that money is the primary requisite
of a candidate. His principles and personality have
very little to do with his success in the election. It

has a most lamentable effect on the quality of the House of Representatives; having very few strong men, its prestige declined. The decline of the lower house in the people's eyes gave an unduly large share of power to the upper house and also to the bureaucracy.

3. There is, in the third place, a singular feature in Japanese politics which arises from expensive elections. It is the fear, or I should say dread, of dissolution on the part of the M.P.'s. Being in a hard-earned position, costing so much, they tremble at the thought of dissolution. This psychology was capitalized by unscrupulous politicians. The Government has the full power to dissolve the House by getting the Emperor's sanction. So, holding this sword above the heads of M.P.'s, it can force almost any number of unpalatable measures on the unwilling members.

This, to my mind, is one of the chief reasons for the great power of the Genro. I should like to avail myself of this opportunity and explain the nature of the world-famous Genro, or elder statesmen of Japan.

The Genro have no official status. Their position has been due to peculiar political conditions of Japan. The late Emperor Meiji used to summon a council of his trusted subjects outside the cabinet to confer with cabinet ministers on grave questions of state. Particularly when a premier resigned and no successor was found, the counsel of these elder statesmen was deemed necessary. The function of the Genro gradually narrowed down to the selection of a new premier.

The selection of a premier is rather simple in such countries as England or France. A man who is sup-

posed to have the support of the majority of the
lower house of Parliament is the one to organize a
cabinet. However, it is not so simple in Japan. One
reason is that the whole political power is not concentrated in the lower house, but a greater reason is,
in my opinion, because a new premier has the absolute power to dissolve the House and by skillful
maneuvers can elect a majority of his own. Okuma
in 1915 dissolved the House and won a tremendous
majority. Terauchi in 1917 dissolved the House and
again won a great majority. I am inclined to at-
tribute the defeat of Kiyoura this year not to his
unpopularity, but rather to his weakness in management and lack of political adroitness.

Such being the situation, the Genro have had quite
a wide field for the selection of premiers. It has not
been necessary for them to recommend the leader of
the majority party or the leader of the opposition.
They have been able to select practically any man
who could by any process organize a cabinet. Therefore when a cabinet crisis comes the attention of the
nation is concentrated on the Genro.

This makes the Genro's position rather strong.
A man ambitious to be premier must be careful not
to incur their displeasure. This also accounts for the
conservative nature of Japanese politics. When
Yamagata was alive, he was practically the whole
Genro. He could make and unmake a cabinet. But
since his death, early in 1922, the power of the Genro
has gradually waned. There is only Prince Saionji
left, and, in the face of the changing social conditions,
he will find it more and more difficult to impose his
own will upon the nation. I think I am pretty safe in

predicting that with Prince Saionji the last of the Genro will pass away.

Then Japan will doubtless resort to the English system of having the outgoing premier recommend the incoming premier. This is not my opinion alone; it is based on the good authority of Mr. Inukai, who has devoted his whole life to the cause of democracy and is a member of the present cabinet.

4. There is another effect of the abnormally large election expenses, *i.e.*, the unavoidable need of every M.P. to recover the money he spent during the campaign. Every M.P. cannot be expected to be a good business man. Hence the unsavory dealings which constitute a great evil of Japan. Corruption during the campaign means corruption after it. The famous sugar scandal of 1910 is a grievous instance.

In all fairness to my own countrymen, I must also tell you that there are a number of sincere reformers who, under heavy disadvantages, have been fighting all these evils, and, thanks to their efforts, brighter days are expected to come.

I must briefly explain here the causes that brought about this unwholesome condition in Japanese politics.

The first and the greatest responsibility falls on the shoulders of the people themselves. They were in the beginning entirely unaccustomed to voting. Therefore they voted as the local bosses told them to; and this created a deplorable situation, namely, the dominance of a class of people who make it their business to organize political machines and squeeze money out of candidates. More blame is to be laid at the door of the educators. They did not give the necessary civic education to the people.

The second reason is more personal. I think the statesmen of Meiji are to be blamed. Yamagata must shoulder a great deal of responsibility for his unscrupulous methods in dealing with party men. Some party leaders were not faultless. Men like Hoshi and Hara cannot escape the reproach of fair critics for their Machiavellian method of promoting party interests.

In the third place, defects in the election law must also be cited. Under the existing law, the control of elections is under the Home Minister, the prefectural governors and the police. It is there that political considerations enter. A new law is under consideration to increase the power of the judiciary so as to make bribing impossible during elections.

However, minute changes in the law of procedure will not be effective in doing away with the political evils which I have just enumerated. The cause lies deeper and the remedy is to come from another source. These great political evils, in my opinion, flowed from the failure of the Meiji Restoration to cultivate the germs of liberalism that sprang up and could not be utterly stamped out by any process. The statesmen of that period restored the Imperial House; they created a strong central government; they saved Japan from falling under foreign domination; but they neglected to emancipate the people. They failed to foresee and prepare for the coming of democracy when they abolished feudal tenures, established a parliament, and made provision for universal education. They ruled the country; they gave the middle class practically no share in the Government; they gave far less to labor. It is by emancipating the middle and working classes that the system of faction and corruption that is so powerful in Japanese politics can be broken down. In this faith I have the example of England. Was not Parliament in the old days of George III dominated by corruption, faction, placemen, and bribery? Does not Macaulay in his wonderful essay on Chatham, show that the remedy lay not in a reduction in the power of Parliament, but in making it responsible to the nation?

III

The coming of the remedy is inevitable. It is at hand. The World War, which really brought about an industrial revolution in Japan, created a large, prosperous, and independent middle class and called into being an active labor movement that cannot be stayed or turned. When the storm broke in August, 1914, Japan little dreamed what a great effect it was destined to have upon her. A temporary business depression was soon followed by a sudden boom and in 1915 practically every factory was humming with work and more work. Coincidently with the material change came another one no less marked. It was the change in political and social ideas.

The new spirit that was gaining ground both in Europe and America rushed into the Island Empire like an avalanche; democracy and liberty were much on the lips of the people. Speeches of the European and American statesmen on the Allied side were followed with intense interest. Mr. Roosevelt and Mr. Lloyd George never failed to arouse enthusiasm. Speeches and messages of President Wilson reached the farthest corners of the Empire.

The liberals at home were not idle. Men like Professors Nitobe and Yoshino were active in disseminating the idea of democracy. The conservatives were frightened and tried to thwart the cause by stamping on it a peculiar brand of "dangerous thoughts." But they little realized that far more dangerous thoughts were being brewed by the changing social conditions, namely, violent socialism and anarchism. By persecuting those who cherished sane ideas of liberalism and democracy, they were driving sensitive, subtle minds further towards the radical cause, which I shall discuss in the next lecture.

The newspapers of the country, with very few exceptions, were on the side of democracy. They, of course, reflected the intellectual currents flowing among the people. Japan in the later years of the World War seemed to make a fair stride towards liberalism and democracy. The prosperous middle class became bolder, and the conservative ruler seemed on the ebbing tide. The sagacious Yamagata was wise enough to read the signs of the times, and was apparently withdrawing his tentacles.

The failure of the democratic leaders of the early days may be traced to many causes. But the predominant reason is attributed by Mr. Inukai to the lack of popular support. He traced this to the fact that those leaders were mostly men who had private axes to grind. They were mainly samurai of Tokugawa affiliations or those of the Tosa and Hizen clans, and they belonged to the same class they fought against. The people found very few economic or moral reasons for supporting them enthusiastically. They were rather in sympathy with the conservatives, who gave them national security and economic prosperity.

But the rising tide of the new liberalism at the end of the World War had an entirely different significance. In the first place, it came from the people. The spread of education gave them more power to think and to understand. Economic prosperity gave them more independence. The increasing power of big capital, the accumulation of which was speeded up by the World War, impressed upon them the vague need of defending themselves by popular representation against the oligarchic rule of the statesmen and big business men and industrialists.

They looked beyond the waters and saw the great drama played in the destruction of oligarchic militarism. Being born on volcanic islands and experiencing earthquakes five times a day, the Japanese are very sensitive. It was the victory of Prussian militarism in 1870 that impressed Yamagata deeply. It was again the intervention of triple powers right after the Sino-Japanese War of 1894-1895 that drove many liberals into the ranks of the imperialists; the most outstanding example being that of Soho Tokutomi, perhaps the greatest journalist of the present-day Japan. Now Japan saw, after a long half-century of conservative ascendancy, the historic rôle of liberalism in a new setting.

The League of Nations made a profound impression on the Japanese. Not only the people in general, but practical politicians began to change their outlook both on internal and international policies. It was a heaven-sent opportunity for the sponsors of democracy in their fight against the conservatives and imperialists. Basing their ideas not on war but on peace, they thought they could build a new social and political policy on a more secure foundation.

When the Washington Conference came, people were in the frame of mind to accept the high principles of the late President Harding. Just before the conference Mr. Yukio Ozaki, the distinguished and consistent exponent of liberalism in Japan, had been on a nation-wide tour pleading for the cause of the limitation of armaments. A straw vote gave him at each meeting over 90 per cent of endorsement. At the session of the Diet following the Washington Conference, both the Seiyukai, the majority party, and the Kakushin Club, a group of progressives, brought out two motions for the same purpose, *i.e.*, the curtailing of the army, which was accepted by the cabinet of the late Admiral Kato and carried out the same year.

The intellectual currents were running even faster than the actual accomplishments in the field of politics. Some sarcastic foreign critics called it Japan's "lip service" to liberalism; but men like Ozaki and Yoshino were exposed to personal risks more than once in pleading for their cause. Some even went to prison for their bold utterances. Groups of literary writers helped to change Japan's thought greatly. I have no time here to deal with the modern literature of Japan. But novelists like Arishima, Tanizaki, Musha-Koji, and Kurata, as well as a poetess like Madam Yosano, are to be thanked for their contributions to the humane and liberal spirit of Japan.

These liberal tendencies are now converging on a definite point—that is, universal manhood suffrage. It is an issue on which the liberalism of Japan is going to have a test. It is quite out of place to tell you all about the conflicts of forces in the past four years. But it is quite probable that the suffrage bill will pass both houses of the Parliament and will become law next winter. That would mean a great stride towards democracy. Japanese internal politics would take on a new phase.

I am strongly inclined here to carry the story into the women's movements in Japan. But I must be very brief. Japanese women enjoyed in the old order a social position which was high and secure. But they had little economic independence and practically no political status in society. The real women's movement in the modern sense dates back only a few decades. Curiously enough, the last national calamity of earthquake and fire gave a tremendous stimulus to that movement. Common suffering and common sympathy drove men and women out of their homes into the open streets to help others. Women of Tokyo of all shades were united in a common cause, and they realized that they were handicapped at all turns on account of their lack of political rights. The advocates of woman's suffrage multiplied. After the universal manhood suffrage bill is passed, the woman suffrage movement will become the next political issue for the liberalism of Japan. Only two years ago the members of Parliament burst out in laughter when one of their colleagues brought up a woman suffrage measure. But they have stopped laughing now. The wind has changed, and they know it.

Another aspect of Japan's liberal tendencies is seen clearly in her changed policy towards China. Japan's "vigorous foreign policy" reached its climax in 1915, when she tendered to Peking the infamous twenty-one demands. Her changing mood appeared first in Paris and then in Washington, and now she has definitely launched upon her new policy, which is called "Japan's Cultural Work in China."

Before I explain this new phase I want to dwell upon a significant incident that happened in China very recently. No doubt you recall the Linshan incident of last year, when Chinese bandits attacked a train of the Tientsin-Poukou Line and carried away many foreigners as hostages.

After this terrible outbreak, a demand was made in Peking that the whole railway system of China should be placed under foreign tutelage. The idea was to set up an organization for this specific purpose, with a Chinese director, and a foreign co-director who was to enjoy equal rights and decide on the matters of railway protection, subject to the approval of the diplomatic corps in Peking.

When this proposal came up in the discussions of the diplomatic corps, Japan voiced her disapproval through her minister, who declared that it infringed upon the sovereign rights of China and was in contradiction to the spirit of the Nine Powers Treaty signed at the Washington Conference. The Japanese view got the support of America and the scheme was finally dropped. China was very grateful for the stand that Japan took on the issue, and there has been no boycotting of Japanese goods this year.

In taking this position, Japan clearly declared her disapproval of the foreign control of China in any form. It is the enunciation of a new policy along liberal lines. Japan was criticised in certain quarters for her refusal to resort to strong medicine for China. But she has firmly made up her mind to live up to the spirit of the Washington Conference, and will stick to the policy of "live and let live" in accordance with the policy of Open Door. We know under what difficulties the Chinese are struggling to bring about peace and unity in that vast country, and they have our whole-hearted sympathy. The underlying thought is expressed eloquently in the words of Baron Shidehara, the present foreign minister, in his first speech in the Diet last July. He said: "We shall watch these efforts of the Chinese people with sympathy, tolerance, and hope, and we pray that they may be crowned with success."

Now I want to explain our so-called "Cultural Work in China." We decided to drop in line with you, although in a little different manner. We are going to use the whole amount of the Boxer indemnity accruing to us from 1922 to 1935 to help advance the civilization and progress of China. The whole sum amounts to seventy-three million yen, or thirty-six and one-half million dollars gold in the ordinary rate of exchange. The first appropriation of 5,350,-000 yen was granted by the July session of the Diet this year. This will be spent in six years for the creation of two Institutes of Research in Peking and Shanghai. The one in Peking will be devoted to research in the field of philosophy, literature, and social science. There will be a large special library attached to it. The other, in Shanghai, will be devoted to research in the field of natural sciences. These institutes are not to be confined merely to the benefit of Chinese and Japanese scholars, but their doors will be wide open to all properly qualified foreigners. The findings of these institutes are to be published in Western languages. This is one of the concrete illustrations of the new policy of Japan in the East.

It must not be thought that this new movement in Japan liberalism is a mere temporary effort to cul-

tivate good will between China and Japan. Cynics
may say that Japan has been forced by the United
States and England to give up her plan for dominat-
ing China, in the interest of a wider distribution of
the spoils. There is, no doubt, some necessity in our
new virtue; such situations are not peculiar to the
Orient. But the new turn in Sino-Japanese relations
has a deeper significance. It is an expression of the
growing desire of the Japanese to take up anew the
study of Oriental civilization. It means that Japan
is discovering that Western civilization, dominated
by the machine and the passion for comfort, offers
no solution to the great problems of inherent permanent national stability, serenity of spirit, and
man's greatest achievement, the conquest of himself.
Triumphant man may not be revealed in the end
adorned in a top hat and attached to a telephone. Asia
has a civilization of her own. To restore and develop
the best in that civilization is a fine work worthy of
the noblest endeavors. So the new *rapprochement*
between Japan and China has a deeper meaning than
is concealed in the bombastic cry of "Asia for the
Asiatics," or "Pan-Asianism." China was there, old
and splendid, when Rome was but a collection of huts
on the banks of the Tiber; Nara, the ancient capital
of Japan, was laid out according to a grand plan
made by skilled engineers in an age when English
London was nothing but a group of rude dwellings
huddled on the banks of the Thames. Perhaps the
people of China and Japan were wrong when they
began to place their hopes on steam engines and par-
liaments alone. Certainly they were wrong when they
thought that machines and test tubes could prevent
wars, revolutions, devastations, and the overthrow of

states and civilization. They must renew their quest, and, in their never-ending search, they are turning once more upon themselves, exploring their own resources of spirit, and seeking a way to victory along paths that are linked to the glories of the past. The tide has set in, deep and irresistible, and those who must gather their understanding of the East from the languages of the West cannot, by any effort, divine its course.

II

THE ORIGIN AND GROWTH OF THE LABOR MOVEMENT IN JAPAN

I

I WANT here to continue to review the social and political changes that are taking place in present-day Japan. As I have told you about, first, the conservative forces and, second, the liberal forces, so I must now discuss the third force that is claiming recognition, *i.e.*, the labor class of Japan.

In the early days of Meiji, Japan was a dreamland of cherry blossoms and beautiful color prints. The Russo-Japanese War changed the scene and Japan came to be regarded as an aggressive power with militaristic designs. In recent years, the viewpoint of the outsider changed once more, and Western people began to ask, "Is social revolution coming to Japan?" Here was a bewildering change of tone, at least to a Japanese. And this is an attempt to answer the latter question.

A comparison of Japan with England helps us in understanding the situation in the former country. In England there are three parties representing, broadly speaking, three different social classes, namely, the Conservative, the Liberal, and the Labor parties. These three parties have come in good historic succession, making the orderly development of the country possible. The English Liberal Party was particularly fortunate in prospering and reaching its goal during the latter half of the nineteenth century. It paved the way for the arrival of another party on the stage, so that a sudden social change which is sometimes fatal to the steady development of the state and civilization was avoided.

Now the social and political development of Japan was destined to be rather different from that of England. When the World War created in Japan a new economic force capable of supporting a real liberal movement strong enough to wage an equal contest with the conservatives, it also caused another force to emerge from the long night of subjection and impotence. Industrial prosperity sent wages soaring to the sky, at least so it seemed to the long underpaid Japanese laborers. Higher wages meant increased power. Japan thus began to have a real labor movement.

The prosperity that the Great War caused was not confined to the industrial laborers. The price of agricultural products also rose, but the increase did not benefit the tenants as much as the landowners. The life of the tenants was made almost unbearable by the rise in the cost of production while no commensurate return was received in the price of their products. This precipitated serious conflicts between the landowners and the tenants. As the tenant class embraces one-third of the whole population of Japan, its profound discontent became a serious menace to the social structure of the country.

How are these different forces, representing different interests, to work out their destinies, and what effects will they have upon the internal and international policies of Japan? The crucial point is whether Japanese liberal forces will be swallowed up by the radical and socialistic forces of labor, or will they be a factor exercising moderating influences upon the rising labor group and lead the country along the path of peace and international good will.

It was under these circumstances that the Immigration Act of your country created so profound a sensation, bringing in its train an invisible but undeniable desire to fall back on Asia. It was all the more impressive because it followed the national calamity of September 1, 1923.

Now let us study the development of the labor movement in Japan.

II

As I have explained, the Restoration of Meiji was necessitated partly by reason of the change that had taken place in the economic fabric of society, *i.e.,* the rise of a commercial class gradually superseding the samurai in wealth and culture. The Restoration was brought about by a combination of insurgent feudal lords against the Shogunate and the big commercial houses. The policy of the Meiji Government tended to favor the growth of business in the towns, which again stimulated the landowners to join the newly organized political parties for the purpose of defending their own interests.

The forty years that followed the Restoration of 1868 saw a gradual industrial revolution taking place in the Island Empire, and by the time of the Russo-Japanese War of 1904-1905 commercial capital had been superseded by industrial capital. With industrial capitalism established we were destined to have the labor problem in the Western sense. And with the labor problem came socialism. The railway men's strike in northern Japan in 1906 and the socialists' conspiracy against the Imperial House in 1910 were the incidents in the changing economic life of Japan that attracted the attention of the people.

In September, 1912, a more significant event occurred. A labor society called Yu-ai-kai was organized, but very few people realized that it was destined to play a great rôle in the future labor movement of Japan. This was the beginning of the organization that developed into the present Japanese Federation of Labor.

Shortly afterward came the World War of 1914-1918, which opened a new epoch for the labor movement of Japan. The business boom in the latter part of the war brought prosperity to industries and wages went up suddenly. The demand for labor was tremendous in 1917 and 1918. It gave working people economic strength as well as a consciousness of power. The social revolution of Russia in 1917 made a great impression on them, too. Now the stage was set and all anxiously waited for the curtain to rise.

The curtain rose in 1919, when strike after strike came in rapid succession, and in the fall of that year labor showed terrifying mass strength in the famous Masmoto affair. This was an organized demonstration of labor protesting against Mr. Masmoto, who had been selected by the Government to represent the Japanese laborers in the first International Labor Conference, held in Washington.

From 1919 to 1921 the labor movement was in the forefront of national attention, but the demands of labor were then more theoretical or legal than economic; that is, labor was more interested in larger social schemes than in hours and wages. The labor leaders demanded the right of collective bargaining, the legalizing of labor unions, and in some cases the control of industries.

The reason can best be understood by turning our attention to the realm of ideas. Now the theories of liberalism and democracy that were gaining ground in Japan during the war reached a climax in 1918 and were destined to be pushed aside or superseded by a more radical scheme of thought, socialism.

Socialism was viewed by the Japanese Government with anything but affection, and particularly after the serious plot of 1910 against the Imperial family it was treated with severity and thus found little room for expression. But after the revolution in Russia and the rapid rise of labor it suddenly began to assert itself in spite of police precautions.

So the Japanese labor movement is marked by peculiarities of its own. In the first place, its appearance was sudden. In the second place, it was hurried forward under the leadership of intellectuals with socialistic affiliations. In the third place, the conditions of the world being so unsettled and revolutionary when it came into existence, it jumped over a number of necessary formative periods instead of advancing step by step. From the stage of prewar suppression it leaped to that of the syndicalist demand for the control of industry. Without going through craft unionism it went right at once to industrial unionism.

This abridgment of the usual course of development was due to the leadership of the intellectuals and particularly the Socialists. It is, therefore, important to trace as fully as time will allow the ideas of these leaders. The history of Japanese socialism can briefly be divided into three periods: the first period, of introduction and education, running from the early days of the Restoration to 1901, when a Social Democratic Party was organized and the movement entered upon the second period—one of action instead of study. This period lasted until 1910, when the intrigue against the Imperial House resulted in the strict prohibition of all socialistic activities in Japan.

After 1910 the Socialists continued their activities in a subterranean manner until the sudden rise of labor to power gave them new opportunities to undertake open agitation. Their contribution to labor's cause was more indirect than direct. They educated the young men who were to be the future leaders of labor.

When Japanese labor entered upon a new epoch of energetic agitation in 1919, its guiding principle was syndicalism. The weapon was direct action and the goal was the control of industry. This phase lasted for about three years and was marked by many strikes of a sensational nature. It gradually changed, however, and by 1922 the idea of syndicalism was supplanted by that of communism.

The conflict of forces in the labor movement came to a crisis on the thirtieth of September, 1922, when the representatives of 136 different labor unions met at Osaka for a national conference. The communists demanded the federation of all labor unions in the country, while the syndicalists opposed them by agitating for the free coöperation of different unions. The meeting broke up in disorder but in reality the victory was won by the communistic elements. This does not mean, however, that Japanese labor became a communist party. It means that Socialists of the communistic school got the ears of the labor leaders, who stood for a close federation of all labor and opposed the loose association idea of the syndicalists.

In those days of syndicalistic and communistic ascendancy, Japanese labor ruled political action out of its programme. The weapon chosen was direct action, and parliamentary activities were despised. Most curiously, the labor leaders of Japan thought that the gentlemen of the Parliament did not represent the real sentiments of the people. And also some of them were under the illusion that a world revolution was on the threshold.

So things stood when the panic of 1920 occurred and as it was followed by an industrial depression it undermined the influence of the theorists. Labor gradually took on a new phase. It had to face the grim, cold fact of unemployment. The nature of strikes changed accordingly. Labor leaders ceased to make theoretical demands and began to make practical demands along economic lines.

Close on the heels of the panic came the earthquake of 1923, which had a profound effect on Japanese labor, particularly the leaders. During the uncertain months immediately following the disaster there was a marked revival of nationalistic sentiments. The assassination of the anarchist leader Osugi by a *gendarme* officer was a manifestation of the violent feeling that existed against radicals of every type. Labor realized that it was not strong enough to carry out its programme single-handed. Then came the announcement of the Yamamoto Cabinet in October that it had decided to introduce the Universal Manhood Suffrage Bill in the coming session of the Diet. This announcement created a sensation all over the country. It made a commotion in the ranks of labor. The chief labor leaders for many years had been against parliamentarism and had ruled all political activities out of their programme. In the moment of their distress and uncertainty a way out was offered to them. They had now to decide whether they would accept the opportunity for enfranchisement and again make use of political institutions as their weapon, or stick to their former plan of direct action. They thus had to decide whether they would coöperate with the liberals in parliamentary action with its slow but steady advance, or continue their friendship with violent socialists of the communistic school.

It is far too soon to make any prediction, but certain facts indicate a changing mood on the part of labor. The Japanese Federation of Labor decided in the autumn of 1923 to create a new branch of political research. The leaders admitted that they were making a study of the advisability of parliamentary action. But I think I am safe in saying that when the Universal Manhood Suffrage Bill is passed in the coming session of the Diet, labor will begin to prepare for the coming election with the idea of sending representatives to the Diet. Although at present the number of organized laborers is only one hundred and fifty thousand against the total number of four millions, I am quite confident that it will increase by leaps and bounds after the passage of the Universal Manhood Suffrage Bill.

Here I may briefly sum up the chronological changes in the guiding principles of the labor leaders. In 1912, when the first labor union was organized under the name of Yu-ai-kai, it was mostly composed of men of liberal tendencies. Gradually it moved on to Christian Socialism, then to Marxism, and in 1919 it switched off to syndicalism. The reign of syndicalism lasted for about three years, when at the general meeting of the labor unions of September 30, 1922, the guiding spirit became communistic.

The earthquake of 1923 and the announcement of the Yamamoto Cabinet in favor of universal manhood suffrage brought another change to their thoughts. The pendulum began to swing back to the right. Labor leaders seem now to be taking the reformist socialists' stand along with the British Labor Party. These changes in opinion must not be construed as the quick movement of the same persons from one principle to another. They were rather due to changes in the personnel of leadership. I am rather inclined to think that with a greater prospect of achievement in the political field and with the illusion of the world revolution dissolved, Japanese labor will come more and more under the influence of liberal, progressive, and practical ideas.

III

The story of the Japanese labor movement cannot be regarded as complete without a survey of the farmers' problem, which has certain features peculiar to Japan. According to the census of October 1, 1920, out of the eleven million families of Japan five and one-half millions were engaged in agriculture; in other words, just about half of the population were farmers. And out of these farmers 70 per cent are to be reckoned as tenants. Although some of this class are petty landowners, their holdings are so small that they are forced to rent additional fields. Japan's agricultural problem is, therefore, a tenant problem.

As the total amount of cultivated land is only about fifteen million acres, one family has only a little less on the average than three acres. But according to the statistics of 1921, the number of families tilling under one and one-quarter acres was 35 per cent of the whole; those tilling between one and one-quarter and two and one-half acres, 33 per cent, and those tilling between two and one-half and five acres 21 per cent; that is to say, nearly 90 per cent of farmers are tilling holdings under five acres. When we look at the ownership of land we find that the acreage of half of the landowners falls under one and one-quarter acres and that those who own 125 acres or more amount to only .09 per cent or four thousand families. About 90 per cent of the landowners fall in the class that owns less than seven and one-half acres.

The most curious phenomenon is that 70 per cent of the owners of land who hold over two acres and a half each are not engaged in actual farming. They belong to the class of absentee landlords. This curious circumstance is the result of the Restoration settlement, which made the position of landowners very favorable. As I have already explained, the political parties of Japan were mainly supported by landowners in the rural districts, and have always been active in advancing their interests. The decrease of the land tax and the increase of farm rent, which on the average amounts to 55 per cent of the yield of the land, made their position rather a comfortable one. Some of the small landowners leased their land and became shopkeepers or salaried employees. But most of the landowners who could eke out an existence preferred to do nothing, and so became an easy-going and indolent class. This gave rise to a deplorable situation in villages, *i.e.,* the existence of two classes—the one working hard and living on the margin of subsistence, and the other leading idle lives and clinging desperately to their farm rents.

But I must not give you a wrong notion of the Japanese peasants by laying stress on the poverty and miserable conditions in which they live, because those who have been in Japan have noticed, I think, that the Japanese peasants, although very poor, are very cheerful and have not lost their sense of humor. Now, the Japanese sense of humor has been questioned very often by foreigners, and in some cases they have even doubted whether the Japanese ever even laughed. This deplorable misunderstanding, I think, is entirely due to the existence of a very high linguistic barrier between the Western peoples and the Japanese. The language of Japan is so difficult for you and your language is just as difficult for us. For instance, I have never seen an American cracking jokes in Japanese. So it is very difficult and even impossible for us Japanese to consciously amuse you in English.

Now, to testify whether there is any sense of humor left in Japan, particularly among the Japanese peasants, I am going to tell you a very good story which in Japan is considered to be the highest type of humor, because it is laconic and pregnant.

In 1878, when local autonomy was given in Japan and Japanese villages began to have assemblies of their own, the population of Japan was not so large as now. The country was sparsely populated. In the

Province of Mikawa, which was named after the three rivers that run through it, there was a village which consisted of only two houses. It happened one day that a traveler was passing through this village and came across a peasant, an old man, sitting on a stone by the roadside. He looked fearfully bored. Curiosity seized the traveler. He went up to the old, and apparently ignorant, peasant and said: "Look here, what's the matter with you? You look so terribly bored." The old man looked up at the traveler with a blank expression in his eyes and answered, "Well, sir, here today I am holding the town meeting."

Now the tenants in Japan are not mere laborers, as are the industrial workers. They are at the same time *entrepreneurs,* bearing the risk of the enterprise. More than that, they are investors in fertilizers and farming implements. The only burden on the landowner is the taxes. It was the tradition of feudalism, making the landowner seem something of a superior being, that caused this condition to endure for so many years after the Restoration of 1868. Gradually, however, the iniquity of the situation became clear and discontent spread among the tenants. Two things helped the growing spirit of unrest among the tenants, *i.e.,* the spread of education and the universal conscription system. In schools and military barracks the sons of the poor tenants for the first time realized that they were the equals of, and in many cases the superiors of, the sons of the rich landowners in physical as well as mental makeup. When they returned to their villages from the military barracks, they could not look upon the sons of men who had been under them in rank in the army as their superiors any more. The field was ready for an outbreak; first, the poverty; then the iniquity of the thing; and, thirdly, the balance of power in favor of the tenants. It only awaited the striking of a match to burst into flame.

The striking of the match came with the Great War of 1914. It sent the prices of industrial products soaring to the sky, while the prices of farm products lagged far behind. Tenants had to pay more for fertilizers and implements, but received little in return for their farm products. The industrial workers in towns were receiving three to four times as much in wages as the tenants. A day came when the latter found that they could not go on any longer. They suddenly arose and demanded the lowering of their rents.

The conflicts between the tenants and landowners were too numerous and too widespread to be reviewed here. In despair the tenants often resorted to violent methods. But they gradually learned that the only effectual way was combination. Collective bargaining began to be adopted as their method. Here their military training began to tell. The discipline they learned in barracks was gradually used to coördinate their action in the economic sphere. The seriousness of the situation impressed the landowners as well as the authorities. Rural problems began to attract the attention of the whole nation.

The organized tenants at first demanded the lowering of farm rents, but this gradually developed into a demand for the emancipation of the land. They contended that landowners have benefited enough from the unearned increment, *i.e.*, the rise in the price of land. There is no reason, therefore, that they should

get any more rent. The right of ownership and the right of use must be separated.

Unlike the laborers in the factories, the farm laborers had some basis for independent action. In the first place, they were the occupants of land and the holders of the products, and they were thus in a position to dictate to the landowners, whereas the industrial workers were the mere recipients of wages. In the second place, the police force is not concentrated in rural districts as it is in cities. In the third place, the tenants could force the hands of landowners by threatening to throw up their holdings, for the owners could find no substitute laborers.

In the opinion of Mr. Toyohiko Kagawa, one of the most prominent social leaders of Japan, the rural development of Japan is in a *cul-de-sac*. He thinks the position of tenants is simply unbearable. According to his researches the tenants are spending 110 yen per one-quarter acre as the cost of production and after paying the farm rent get only 105 yen, *i.e.,* five yen less than they actually spend. They make this deficiency good by turning out some by-products, like silk or eggs. Meanwhile the larger landowners are living in the big cities and spending their unearned income in luxuries. In his opinion the only way out of the *impasse* is to do away with private undertakings, resort to a coöperative system of management, and gradually buy up the land from the owners.

However, it is not fair to lay all the blame on the shoulders of landowners. The fact is, in Japan agriculture has become too difficult to be a profitable undertaking. Both the landowners and the tenants are losing their interest in agriculture. They would be only too happy to leave the farm if they could. Here is the seriousness of the problem. In a word, we are up against a great stone wall—the scarcity of land in proportion to population. There are only three ways out of the *impasse*. We must either increase our landholdings, decrease our population, or industrialize the whole country. This, however, is too large a question to be dealt with here.

Now I should like to inquire in what way the tenant problem is going to affect the politics of Japan and eventually her diplomacy.

The outstanding feature of the Japanese tenants' theories is that they are entirely indigenous and have not been influenced by any foreign ideas, as have the labor doctrines of the industrial workers in cities. Therefore the former are not definitely socialistic as are the latter. What the tenants demand is not the abolition of the ownership of the landlord; but rather the free use of the land.

In the second place, they have been and are in better position politically. They can force their will more easily upon the Government than can the industrial workers. The new town and village law of 1920 and the prefectural laws of 1921 emancipated practically all the peasants politically. There is, it is true, a property qualification in the new laws. But the provisions enfranchise all taxpayers and do not fix any minimum amount. Theoretically speaking, a taxpayer of one single sen is qualified to vote for the village and prefectural assemblymen. It means universal manhood suffrage for local elections. And the peasants were not slow in using the new weapon. They captured the village assemblies in a number of places and have returned some representatives to prefectural assemblies. They are now waiting for the passing of the universal manhood suffrage bill for the Diet. Then they will try to elect their own representatives to the national Parliament.

The Japanese local elections and national elections are very interesting for outsiders to study because of the humorous side. During the elections we have a great deal of hot-air speech from soap boxes, and if you could attend one of those assemblies you would be highly amused to witness the phenomenon. The orators are all heckled heartily by the audiences, which is highly amusing—I mean for the audience. That shows that Japanese peasants are not slow in taking advantage of occasions to have their good laugh. I think I can explain it by telling you a good joke on me. During the last election I had the misfortune to run for a seat in the Diet, and during the campaign my opponent did his best to attack me personally. In one of the villages, where about sixty peasants, not very well educated, very innocent, unsophisticated, were attending a meeting of my opponent, one of the gentlemen who were boosting my opponent took the platform and said:

"Now, our opponent says that there are two good reasons for recommending that fellow by the name of Tsurumi. One is that he has traveled extensively in Europe and America. Well, gentlemen, if traveling in Europe is one of the best qualifications to be an M.P., why not select one of the captains of the ocean liners of the Japan Steamship Company? And the second reason for boosting Tsurumi is said to be that he can speak English rather well. Well, if that is a qualification, why not pick up one of the interpreters in one of the harbors, like Yokohama? But the gentleman whom I am going to present before you today is of a different sort entirely. Instead of going abroad so many times, and instead of wasting his time in the study of a foolish language like English, he has been since his graduation from the University working in the rice field as a common peasant.''

Then all of a sudden one of the old peasants stood up and said, ''Well, sir, if that is the best qualification to be an M.P., I think we are all better qualified, because we have all been working in the rice fields since boyhood and we didn't go to any university, either.''

As I have already explained, the mainstay of the Japanese political parties has been in the rural districts, where the voters were mainly landowners. So the parties represented the interests of the landowners as against the tenants. It is no wonder that the latter are not particularly in love with the parties. In fact, there is a growing tendency among the active and spirited tenants to oppose all the existing parties.

Does this mean then that the tenants will combine or at least coöperate with the urban laborers and organize a new party? That is a most perplexing and interesting point. Even a distinguished labor leader admitted to me its difficulty. And in the opinion of a prominent student of the tenant problem, the tendency seems to be in the opposite direction. In the light of the little experience I had in the last election, I am inclined to think that the tenants will rather support a progressive liberal than a socialistic radical. Although economic necessity has driven them in recent years to more or less radical methods, they are at heart more conservative by nature of their occupation. I am inclined to think that Japanese peasants are hard-headed and little given to radical ideas. As it was they who helped the Meiji Restoration to work out its destiny and purpose, so again it may be their lot to bridge over the gulf during crucial periods of transition and help lead the nation along a peaceful road. In a word, if the public men of Japan do not make blunders, the peasants of Japan will be the mainstay of the future liberalism of Japan, counterbalancing the socialistic tendencies of the urban laborers.

IV

Now let me consider briefly the bearing of these labor and tenant movements on international affairs. I will take as an example their policy towards the recent Immigration Law of America. The Japanese Federation of Labor did not issue any public statement on the question, so the outside world does not know what its stand really is. If I am allowed to reveal the inside story, I may say that there has been a pretty hot discussion among the leaders of the Japanese Federation of Labor. One party insisted on issuing a protest over their own names on grounds of humanity, while another party contended that as the immigration policy is purely a matter of economic interest, America had the right to decide as she pleased. The reasoning of this latter party runs as follows: The fundamental question was settled in 1907, when Japan surrendered her right to send immigrants to the United States, and the recent Immigration Law makes no economic change. The cry of "national honor" and "humanity" is entirely sentimental and has no relation whatever to any significant economic interest. The immigration policy of America is perfectly natural so long as capitalism and nationalism rule in this world. A protest could be justified only if it is made to the American Federation of Labor, and if the rumor is true that American labor helped to pass the bill. If so, American labor has followed in the steps of capitalists and is not living up to the accepted principles of the international labor movement. It is best that we do not protest at all. This opinion was accepted and the Japanese Federation of Labor made no public statement of policy on the Immigration Bill.

Now this is the important point to which I want to call your attention. This is where the liberal and socialistic standpoints differ. The socialist does not believe in the present system of the national government based on private ownership, and to him the Immigration Bill is only a good example of the failure of a capitalistic government to deal with a vital question of the day. So to him it is not worth while to protest. A liberal believes in the present system of government, and also believes that conflicts among nations can be solved without radical changes in the national government and in private ownership.

The socialist views the world from the standpoint of sheer economic interest and the liberal recognizes a place for honor and sentiment in all kinds of human activities. To a socialist the exclusion clause of 1924 is nothing, because it does not affect Japan's economic interests in the matter, which were surrendered in 1907 by the "gentlemen's agreement." A liberal protests against the exclusion clause because it implies the lack of confidence in the Japanese nation, which had given its word of honor not to send any immigrants and has lived up to its agreement faithfully.

The upshot of the matter, therefore, is this: The Immigration Bill tends to drive a wedge between labor and liberalism, and to turn labor more and more to Russia. Japanese labor leaders are saying that the Immigration Act merely proves the folly of cultivating sentimental relations with capitalistic America and the importance of entering into close and binding relations with socialist Russia, with a view to the development of mutual economic interests on the Asiatic mainland. Such a movement might very well be executed in the beginning under imperialistic auspices; it might make use of nationalistic devices as defensive weapons against all outside interference. It would inevitably lead to the concentration of Japanese efforts upon Asiatic combinations and weaken the forces that work for liberal and democratic institutions in Japan. Already labor leaders are telling us that British and American democracy is an illusion that hides ruthless capitalism, and that the sooner Japan turns her back upon that delusion the better for the welfare of her people. Thus it becomes as difficult for a Japanese liberal to influence Japanese labor as to convince the hardened nationalist that America sincerely desires permanent and cordial peace with the Japanese nation.

Now let us turn to the reaction on the tenants. The Japanese farmers gave up the hope of migrating into the United States long ago. They are not interested in American immigration, but they are keenly interested in emigration. They know that the situation of the Japanese farmers is unbearable. They are casting about for a way out, and I think I am not very much mistaken in saying that they are more and more interested in Siberia.

Here I am entering upon a new phase of my story, *i.e.,* Japan's relationship to Russia. Not having enough space at my disposal, I must satisfy myself by just telling the conclusion. American policy in the last few years has been driving Japan towards Russia and the recent Immigration Law still hastened the tendency, among the laborers and tenants. They felt that Japan had been turning her face too long towards America and that it was high time that she should reverse it.

Is it necessary for me to summarize? Is it not evident that the grave consequences to which I refer inhere in the possible separation of the labor movement and the agrarian movement from the forces of liberalism? For those already versed in the political and economic history of the past three hundred years, it is not necessary for me to complete the picture. The dim outlines upon the screen are enough for those who are interested in maintaining the peace of the world and the orderly development of society.

Japan has in recent years been called by some critics a menace to the peace of the world. They little realized Japan's contribution to the stability of the Far East. Without Japan the Balkanization of China might have occurred, adding another store of explosives to the great danger of existing society. People failed to divine the danger that was lurking underneath the apparent tranquillity of the East.

The long night of the Orient is destined to end. The dawn is at hand. An industrial revolution has been preparing for the rising of the new sun. When the white lights of the morn fall on the woods and rivers and hills and dales, and the rustling of leaves and the twittering of birds are heard in suppressed undertones of dreamlike mystery, who knows then that in the cities and villages from the Pacific to the Indian Ocean the human mind is not astir? The teeming millions of Asia will wake up one day from the silent slumber of centuries. Murmuring is already heard in Bombay, Canton, and Osaka. Who can deny, then, that the guiding principle and policies of the laboring people of Japan will wield an irresistible influence on the social destiny of the whole Orient?

I. ECONOMIC RECOVERY IN THE WORLD

II. ECONOMIC CONFLICTS AS THE CAUSES
    OF WAR

BY SIR JAMES ARTHUR SALTER

I

ECONOMIC RECOVERY IN THE WORLD

In the five years that have passed since the conclusion of the Great War, of all the subjects which have occupied the attention and anxious concern of the world, whether it be wars and threats of wars, pestilences, social revolutions, elections, or the fate of our favorite baseball team, the most universal and absorbing question of world interest has been the world's economic recovery. During this period we have had a series of attempts to appreciate the position, to diagnose the trouble, to prophesy the future. These attempts have been made under great, but I think now diminishing, difficulties. They have varied from a natural, but excessive, optimism during the period of postwar boom and inflation to what I think, and have always thought, the equally excessive pessimism of the painful period of deflation and depression. It has taken some time for the more permanent and vital factors to disengage themselves from the trivial and the temporary.

I think that the moment for a new attempt has now arrived. Ten years have now elapsed—ten years this very day—since the economic life of the world was forced to adapt itself, suddenly and violently, to the new needs of a great war; for nearly six years the reverse process of readjustment to the needs of peace has been in operation. This second readjustment, slower and in some respects more difficult, has encountered many obstacles. The moment when the greatest of these—the weight of an indefinite and unsettled reparation obligation—is, as we all hope, now being removed by the unanimous adoption and the application of the Dawes Report, is an appropriate one at which to attempt a survey of progress already attained.

I can myself make only a slight contribution to such an attempt, particularly in the short time that is available today. I have had the advantage, during the last few years, of a convenient observation post in my office at Geneva. In the vast and intricate struggle towards economic recovery which is taking place throughout Europe, we have from Geneva taken no inconsiderable part. But the field of action which we attempt to survey is much wider than that which we ourselves in any way control, and in what I have to say I shall refer to the specific work of the League only in its due place as a part of the much greater movement of reconstruction—whether by national, international, or individual effort—throughout the Continent. On a subject so vast, and in space so limited, I can only convey a very general—and personal—impression. I hope, however, that what I say may provoke a more serious attempt at analysis and diagnosis by more authoritative students.

It is interesting, in looking back over the last five years, to see how differently the main economic trouble has been diagnosed; to see how, at different periods, one cause after another has been, in international conferences and by the most authoritative expert opinion, considered the most serious and the most fundamental obstacle to recovery; and how one after another these causes have lost their importance. In saying this I do not suggest that the most authoritative expert opinion was wrong. Sometimes certainly, for the time, it was right. Sometimes perhaps the very insistence upon the seriousness of a particular trouble helped to terminate it. But it is certainly curious to notice how different any diagnosis made now is, and must be, from those of a few years ago. A rapid review of the incorrect or obsolete explanations will, I think, help to guide us to the true one. Let me summarize them briefly.

I well remember that during the Peace Conference the gravest fear for the future was that of the spread of what was called, sometimes loosely, sometimes more exactly, "Bolshevism." Sometimes what was feared was the actual adoption by other countries of the political and economic doctrines then in force in Russia. Sometimes it was something more general and less specific than this. We wondered whether after four years of war the ordinary man would ever again be willing to return to the arduous and monotonous routine of his prewar work; whether he would not insist upon such radical changes in the conditions of his work or remuneration as would render an adequate production impossible. There was, indeed, as a reaction from the strain and effort of the war a wave of what Mr. Hoover called "demoralized productivity" throughout all countries— and I may add all classes, though, fortunately for many of us, our individual work is not capable of such exact measurement as that of a miner who hews a ton of coal out of the earth. No one knew how serious or how durable this undoubtedly real phenomenon of slackness and unsettlement would be. It certainly increased and confirmed the fears of those who thought that the very bases on which a civilized

standard of life must be maintained were tottering
and perhaps destined to fall.

Well, we may perhaps now say with confidence
that that danger and that trouble are past. They may
of course return; but they are no serious factor in
the present position or the reasonably near future.
"Bolshevism" (a term which I here use in its economic rather than its political connotations), in the
sense in which it was a subject of active terror in
1919, has not spread from Russia to other countries;
and in Russia itself it is apparently being modified
into a formless destructive to production and perhaps
to commerce. And generally speaking, throughout
the world—not excepting Russia—the ordinary man
desires nothing better than a reasonable day's pay
in return for a reasonable day's work. I hasten to
add that I do not, by this, mean that we all work as
hard as we might. We never did: we never shall. But
I do mean that as an explanation of the specific
economic troubles of the present an increased disinclination to work or to accept the conditions essential to adequate production as compared with the
prewar period is no longer a serious factor.

At the same period, but with less justification and
less authoritatively, the opinion was held by many
persons that among the most serious obstacles to
recovery was, and was likely to be, a shortage of
mercantile ships through the destruction by the sub-
marines. This was a popular error gaining some
color from obviously temporary factors which should
never have deceived (as they did) serious economic
observers. During the war the shortage of ships had,
as everyone knew, brought the whole Allied cause
near disaster. And immediately after the war several

special causes kept freights high. The troops had to be repatriated. Food had to be rushed into starving countries. Raw materials for reconstruction and for the restarting industries were also in exceptional demand. Most important of all, the temporary slackness of work caused delays in port—in fact, the reduction in the world's transporting capacity due to port delays was for a time greater than that due to all the loss of tonnage during the war. These were all temporary—and should have been seen to be temporary—causes. It was not long before shipping was a drug on the market, before two million tons of shipping were held up in British ports, not because of slackness in loading or discharging them, but because there was no work for them to do. Only yesterday I saw on the Hudson, halfway between here and New York, a fleet of fine, large cargo ships tied up idle and apparently having remained for a long time idle. I knew that there were many others elsewhere, both in America and the rest of the world. My mind turned back six or seven years, when Mr. Rublee and Mr. Morrow and myself were engaged in the common problem of trying to find ships for cargoes that could not be carried; and even a little further back than that, seven years back, when I was sent by the British Government to urge upon the American Government what was then only too desperate a truth, that there was nothing in the world so valuable to the Allied cause as merchant shipping.

I remember a year later, when America by an almost, perhaps a quite unparalleled feat of engineering, was turning out great numbers of ships from Hog Island—I remember watching the progress of the output by records in London day by day,

when every ship seemed to carry the fate of the
Allied cause with it. And now, so short a time after,
you have those ships lying there, as in many other
parts of the world. So do the needs of the world
change.

The next trouble to which attention was directed
was an alleged shortage of raw materials. If you
look up the records of international conferences—
whether the Supreme Economic Council at Paris, the
meetings of the Council of the League at Geneva and
elsewhere, the Brussels Financial Conference, and
the series of Allied conferences from Spa to Genoa,
you will find constantly recurring schemes for the
rationing and distribution of raw materials, based
on a shortage anticipated to be permanent or of long
duration. That trouble too has long disappeared from
the anxieties of manufacturers and from the agenda
of conferences. There has long been an adequate
supply of all raw materials for every effective economic demand. The discussions of rationing schemes
already seem part of a past era.

Others, including many serious observers, thought
the trouble was even wider and deeper. They wondered whether, after the destruction and disorganization of the war, the world's capacity of production
was adequate to support a reasonable standard of
life. It was said that the population of Europe ex-
ceeded the number which Europe's own production
(whether for direct consumption or in exchange for
foreign produce) could support. Estimates of this
kind were based on a curious misunderstanding of
what had really been happening in the war. The
merely financial arrangements for the distribution
of wealth through loan operations disguised the fact

that the enormous bulk of what was being consumed and destroyed during the war was, of necessity, also produced during the war and drawn neither from past riches nor future production. In the ultimate and material sense, posterity cannot be made to pay for a war. It is fortunate indeed that the shell which is to be fired today must have been made yesterday and cannot be made tomorrow; and that the great bulk of the accumulated real capital of the past cannot, for physical reasons, be consumed in war. Properly considered, the experience of the war showed two things: first, the relatively small proportion which the destruction of previous wealth bore to current production, and, secondly, the large margin of the world's productive capacity beyond the needs of a reasonable standard of life. I venture to quote the following passage from a work of my own (*Allied Shipping Control*) as to war production during the war in Great Britain:

At a moderate estimate, and allowing for the production of persons who were idle before the war, between half and two-thirds of the productive capacity of Great Britain was withdrawn into combatant or other war service. And yet throughout the war Great Britain sustained the whole of her military effort and maintained her civilian population at a standard of life which was never intolerably low, and for some periods and for some classes was perhaps as comfortable as in time of peace. She did this without, on balance, drawing any aid from other countries. She imported, on borrowed money, less from America than she supplied, on loaned money, to her Allies. She therefore maintained the whole of the current consumption both of her war effort and of her civilian population with a mere remnant of her productive power by means of current production. The only exception to this general statement is the extent to which she used up existing capital; and she only did this in so far as foreign securities were sold and the net real capital of the country deteriorated (in the form of unrepaired and unrenewed houses, roads, railways, etc.) to a value exceeding any gain through new capital and plant constructed in the war and still remaining useful after it. The loans she raised from her people are, of course, no deduction from this general statement, as internal loans merely represent a method of taxation and not a method of doing what is essentially impossible, that is, making the production of a later age available for the consumption of the present. The general and amazing fact therefore remains, without essential qualification, that with more than half her productive capacity withdrawn, Great Britain met the scarcely diminished necessities of her civilian population by current production.

I need only add that in speaking not of a single country but of the world as a whole, such a statement needs even less qualification. The sale of securities and external as well as internal loans means only a redistribution of wealth and not a reduction. The actual physical diminution of the wealth and real, material capital of the world by the war, was a very small proportion indeed either of its accumulations or its current production.

Lastly, among the fundamental obstacles to recovery, great importance was attached—from the Supreme Economic Council of 1919 down to the Genoa Conference of 1922—to the inadequacy of the railways. The blocking of transport was thought to be the bottle-neck of the economic system. For a time, indeed, and especially during the inflationary boom of 1920, it was so. It has definitely ceased to be so now. We have recently had a general survey of the whole European railway system by a League expert. His report is conclusive. With the important exception of Russia, and some minor exceptions of no great importance, the railway system is practically back to prewar standards; in any case, it is not the limiting factor in economic recovery. Improvement would doubtless assist economic development, as it always has and will; but any imperfections are no serious obstacle to recovery. In general, the transport system is adequate to the traffic it is asked to bear. Here again, almost before discussions of how the repair of the transport system of Europe could best be effected, trains were beginning to run empty because the new deflationary period had robbed them of their freights.

Here, then, are the incorrect and obsolete diagnoses of the past. What is the true one? What is it that is really, through large parts of the world, causing unemployment, impoverishment, or a reduced standard of life?

Of course, there is no single cause. There are many. But do these causes fall within any general description? Can we with reasonable exactness describe the economic trouble of the world in a single, if rather general, formula? I think we can.

What is wrong is not inadequate resources, or inadequate effort; it is all, in one form or another, *a misdirection of effort*. There is a maladjustment, seriously greater than before the war, between supply and demand. The links between producer and consumer have been broken. The processes by which the wealth of different countries—and different individuals—is exchanged have, by comparison with the prewar position, been arrested, impeded, broken, and restricted. Production is in some countries starved of working capital. This is not because the world's margin of production over consumption is not sufficient to provide capital. It is because in the countries most in need of capital the inducements to save have been destroyed or diminished by a depreciating exchange; and the countries which have spare capital are loth to lend it to the others for similar reasons. A misdirection of effort; a maladjustment of supply and demand, a sense of insecurity, diminishing savings, and impeding their use where they are most wanted as working capital: *i.e.*, a disorganization of the system of credit, a restriction of the range of international commerce. This is what is wrong, and practically the whole of what is wrong. It is indeed enough, but it is much less than has till recently been generally believed. We must, of course, examine these general causes rather more closely.

But before we become more specific, let us turn for a moment to first principles. The total wealth of the world, and the practicable standard of life for a given total population, is the combined net result of three factors: the resources of nature; the capacity of man to exploit them; and a system which enables the specialized product of one country, one region, or one individual to be exchanged for that of another. Now the resources of nature remain the same. The capacity of man to exploit them increases continually. What has gone wrong is that the system which enables one product to be exchanged for another throughout the world has been in a hundred forms interfered with, interrupted, arrested.

Till the outbreak of war the range and efficacy of

the system of interchange had been no less notably increasing. The improvement in transport and in communications, the gradually built-up trade connections throughout the world, the elaboration and extension of financial operations, the sense of security in the will and power to execute long-term contracts, the existence of a single effective currency throughout the great part of the world (for all currencies based on gold, however expressed in national denominations, were in effect a single currency)— all tended to the same effect. All meant that to a constantly increasing extent the individual in all countries could find for his specialized skill a world market and for his needs could call upon the ends of the earth. And every new increase in the range, ease, and cheapness of this interchange was just as certainly an increase in the total general wealth of the world—and a factor in raising standards of living —as an invention which actually increased or cheapened production. When the war broke out the general level of prosperity reflected the net result of this improvement in the range and ease of interchange just as much as the improvement in the processes of production; and the population of the world had increased up to the resources so made available. It is here, and here only, that the process has been arrested and reversed. The resources of nature remain, the capacity of man to exploit them is still increasing. But, in a hundred ways, the war has blocked, impeded, or broken the system of interchange, always with net loss of consumable wealth. If any lesson has been vividly enforced during the last few years it is surely the essential interdependence of all the countries of the world upon each other's respective prosperity. If any country, by internal trouble, such as revolution, or natural disaster or external action, such as pestilence or earthquakes, or by some combination of all of these, is separated from the general economy of the world, the result is, with mathematical certainty, material loss not only to its own inhabitants, but to the rest of the world as a whole. I say as a whole advisedly, because it is of course true that particular classes, even in a special case a given country, may gain more from the disappearance of a competitor than they would lose either in a market or as a purchasing consumer. But always, as a whole, the world must lose in the net and total result. And what is true in the almost theoretical case of the complete disappearance of a country from the world's economy is of course true *pro tanto* of every reduction or restriction of interchange, of which recent experience affords only too many examples. Whenever the fluctuations of exchange, or apprehensions of internal disorder or external conflict, or official restrictions and prohibitions, or the mere severance of old trade connections, or change of national habits of trade, restrict the range of international commerce, the result is, and must always be, the same; some individuals may snatch a profit, but the world as a whole *must* lose. Our present troubles, from which the richest countries are not exempt, are the net result of this process—operating in many forms. It is beyond argument or reasonable dispute, in the interest of the world as a whole, that with the aid of peace, both internal and external, the financial and economic conditions of all countries should be such as to encourage both production and a frictionless interchange of their products.

These are, however, generalities, and perhaps platitudes—if what is only recognized in theory and not translated into practice remains only a platitude. Let us be more specific.

There are, of course, many factors in this restriction of interchange—in the disturbance of the adjustment of supply and demand. There are inappropriate or cumbersome official regulations, increased or changing customs duties, the severance of established trade connections, friction in the adjusting system of prices whether arising both from employers' monopolies or Trade Union restrictions, and others. But the most important of the difficulties find either their expression or their cause in fluctuating monetary exchanges; and on these, therefore, I propose to enlarge a little. Speaking in a country which has not known from personal experience within living memory what the troubles of a fluctuating and falling domestic currency are, I should like to interpose a few words to try to make vivid what is the extraordinary difference in the situation of those countries in Europe where the exchange has been going to pieces. Here, happily, in America, the foreign exchanges are a subject of interest to bankers, to foreign merchants, to tourists and travelers to other countries, and only to those. In many countries of Europe a falling foreign exchange is a subject of the most intimate and important concern for the daily life of every class. I well remember how this was brought home to me some three or four years ago, when I happened to be in Saarbrück, one of the chief towns in the little but famous Saar coal basin between France and Germany. I saw outside the town hall some huge blackboards, and as I got nearer I saw that these blackboards showed the foreign exchange quotations of the day, the franc and the mark and the other currencies. Before these blackboards I saw six or seven washerwomen with their baskets of washing on their arms, studying the rates of foreign exchange for the day. That was not because there was an exceptional degree of scientific interest in the washerwomen of that part of Europe. It was because the movement of those exchanges affected the daily domestic life of those women as of everyone in that country. It meant a difference in what they could buy with the wages they earned in one country in articles which came from another. Happy indeed is the country that is unconscious of its foreign exchange.

Let me give one more example. Before the war it used to be a favorite device of a particular type of novelist to illustrate the reckless extravagance of a hero by saying that he used a bank note to light his cigar with. There have been many times in many places in Europe when a bank note has been literally the cheapest form of pipe lighter. I remember in the autumn of 1922, when the League of Nations was first beginning to take up the case of Austria, I had a small staff of clerks in Vienna, and I went into their room one day and noticed that they were using a rather peculiar block of writing paper for rough notes. I picked it up and found it consisted of one-crown Austrian notes, and I was told that there was no way of getting scrap paper that was anything like so economical. So that the very symbol of reckless extravagance has become a measure of prudent economy.

But in passing I would like to use the same example

to illustrate one other result of a fluctuating and falling exchange. I looked at that note, that one-crown note, to see the date on which it had been purchased. I found that it bore a recent date, June, 1922. I took the trouble to find what it cost in Austrian crowns to print a note, the paper and the printing, of that date. It cost nearly ninety crowns. Consider the state of disorganization of a country which continues to print bank notes when it costs ninety of those bank notes to pay for one.

I said just now that most of the cases that are interrupting and impeding international commerce find either their cause or their expression in fluctuating exchange. I said "either their cause or their expression" advisedly, for this reason: A fluctuating exchange or a falling exchange is practically always a symptom of deeper troubles. It is a great mistake to look upon inflation as a mere vice, a sort of post-war finance ministers' drug habit, which in all cases should, and could, have been avoided. The fact is that just as there were real, if varying and elastic, limits to the power of governments during the war to finance their war expenditure by taxation without loans, so there have been real limits to the power of many of them to finance their postwar expenditure for unavoidable needs by taxation and real loans without inflation. Inflation has been as inevitable for many countries as war loans were. Objectionable as it is in many respects as a form of taxation, it was often the only politically practicable method of obtaining the resources without which there must have been social collapse. In many countries the dead weight of government debt was an impossibly heavy load upon their economic life, and overt repudiation would have been politically impracticable and financially more disastrous than temporary inflation. But it is equally clear that if such inflation has many great advantages during a short transition period, they are essentially temporary. In time inflation fails even in its primary purpose of giving the Government the resources it needs; and after an equally limited period, during which it has the same stimulating effect on industry as the discovery of a new gold mine has under the orthodox system, it is necessarily destructive of international commerce. For international commerce, particularly between distant countries, needs above all things a stable medium. And the fatal thing about a policy of inflation is that it is so difficult to stop. It involves drastic legislative and financial measures which are too often politically impossible under the ordinary working of a democratic constitution. This is why we have seen that Austria and Hungary alike have needed the stiffening of international coöperation and control. In other countries, such as Italy, where an internal national effort has met with some success, it has been through the replacement of the ordinary democratic system by a more dictatorial form of government. In countries such as Germany and France, where reparation payments and receipts are important items in the budget, a stable exchange is practically impossible while they remain unknown and uncertain. For exchange cannot remain stable unless the national budget is balanced, and while there is a reasonable confidence that it will remain balanced. And while it is difficult enough to raise taxes for a certainty, it is always politically impossible to raise them for needs that remain the subject of uncertain estimate or speculation.

What, therefore, we need in order to remedy the fluctuation of exchanges is in some cases the continuance of such international efforts as are being made in Austria and Hungary; in others the successful completion of national efforts, such as we see in Czechoslovakia, Italy, and more recently in Poland; and, above all, the removal—let us hope now in sight by the adoption of the Dawes Report—of the great element of uncertainty in the financial estimates of some of the main countries of Europe—an unsettled reparation obligation. The conditions will then exist on which the uncertainties of the exchanges can be ended, or reduced within harmless limits.

I have no time now to go into the technical means by which this result may be achieved. I hope to have a later opportunity. But I would like to emphasize that the object to be aimed at is simply *stability*. It is not, of course, a restoration of national currencies to their prewar values. Such a policy would be alike disastrous and impracticable in all cases where the currency has very considerably depreciated. It would make the burden of internal debt intolerable and in the process of application would alike disorganize the economic life of the country. Stability must be secured by arresting depreciation, not reversing it. Devaluation is in most cases the necessary complement of stabilization.

Let me explain that a moment. Let us imagine that the national expenditure of a given country is, say, one hundred millions of its national unit, whatever it is. Let us imagine that fifty millions of this goes to pay the actual charges on internal, mostly war, debts.

Let us imagine, thirdly, that this currency is worth half its standard prewar value in terms of gold. What would be the result, supposing the Government of that country said, "We are going to get that currency back to its prewar value, that is to say, to double its present value"? That would mean in future, when they succeeded in that process, every bank note of that country would purchase twice as much as at present. By necessary consequence the average income would in terms of those bank notes be half what it is at present. The consequence of that would be that the receipts of taxation (again in terms of those same notes) would be half what is at present obtained. Consequently the country would be getting fifty millions instead of its present one hundred. But it has to pay fifty millions to meet its internal war debt. That fifty millions could remain fifty millions, and therefore the whole resources of taxation would go towards meeting that internal debt, leaving nothing for the current expenditures of the Government.

Now, as the very reason why the exchange has fallen in the past has been that the Government has not been able to increase the rate of its taxation, it is quite obvious that the Government could not remedy the situation by increasing its taxes. Moreover, think of the social and economic trouble that would be involved during the process of achieving that result. When you have to drive down wages to half their nominal value, it is quite true that theoretically, and in the long result really, those half wages would buy as much as the full wages used to before. But you would have some difficulty in strikes and other ways before you could get that theory accepted at the time when you were putting that operation into practice. That is why, in my view, when you have had an immense depreciation in currency, a return to a prewar standard is practically impossible.

And stability is required in two directions. To serve its essential purpose in the internal economic life of a country, the probable variations in value of the national currency in terms of commodities, that is, its purchasing power, must be reduced to reasonable limits. Which of these two aims a country should have primarily in view—whether a reversion to a revised gold basis, like through direct convertibility into gold or some form of gold exchange system, or whether a different basis shall be sought—is a question needing more time than is available. All I can now do is to emphasize that in any event the object is a reasonable, not absolute, stability in value; a sufficient stability to encourage saving, to attract investments of both domestic and foreign capital, and to serve as the basis of long period contracts.

The present instability of the exchanges is of course very closely associated with the other main root of the present economic troubles—the disorganization of the credit system. The maintenance of production and the present standards of life means not only that capital must be renewed: it must be increased proportionately to the increase in population. Now currency depreciation commonly has three results: First, it leads a country, even unconsciously, to draw on its real capital, for the reductions in real value are disguised by the nominal increases in terms of currency; secondly, it discourages the formation of capital by saving, for if savings are likely to lose most of their value the inducements to immediate consumption are irresistible; and, thirdly, it destroys the basis of confidence and security in which alone it is possible for the capital available in countries where there is a margin to be used in others where industry most needs it.

I have said that currency depreciation discourages saving and I would like to illustrate that by an example. In Austria, some years ago, a wealthy father died and left his two sons his fortune in equal shares. One of those sons was a prodigal and a spendthrift; the other was an extremely cautious and careful and economical person. The first of those two sons spent the whole of his half share of the fortune in riotous living, very largely upon champagne. The second, the prudent son, put the whole of his half share into Austrian national bonds. In the course of two or three years the mere empty champagne bottles were worth more than the crowns which the bonds purported to represent.

You will understand, therefore, that a falling, fluctuating currency is a discouragement to prudent investments. I do not mean to suggest that that is the case with most of the investments to which the American investor is asked at the present time to subscribe to in Europe.

Behind and below the instability of currencies and the disorganization of credit, there are, of course, as a fundamental factor of the first importance, the prospects of war and peace. There is, first of all, the actual financial burden which the prospect of war invokes, the burden of armaments, which accounts for a serious item in all national budgets and a dominant one in some of those least able to sustain it. In even a moderate example you may find no less than

75 per cent of the proceeds of taxation devoted either to paying for past wars or preparing for future ones. The greater part of this, of course, is payment for the past and therefore irrevocable, but for many countries in Europe where the sense of security is least, and where the difficulties of securing budget equilibrium are greatest, the actual cost of current armaments is a decisive item in the country's finances. I do not wish to overstress this. We cannot say that for Europe, or for the world as a whole, the real burden of armament expenditure is greater than before the war; and we cannot therefore put it as a principal cause in accounting for present impoverishment in comparison with the prewar period. More important than actual military expenditure is the reaction of a sense of insecurity upon the economic processes of the world.

What the world needs, in order to regain and extend the wide range of frictionless interchange of its productions and with it the recovery of its prosperity, is above all peace and the assurance of peace. In a world psychology in which the apprehension of war remains a primary complex, the economic life of the world will necessarily tend to shrink into separate, impoverished, defensive systems. Confidence alone can stimulate enterprise and extend its range.

But assuming that by the deliberate and combined efforts of the great countries of the world, in whatever form it is put, peace and confidence in peace can be assured, I cannot refrain from expressing now an optimistic opinion as to the general prospects of economic recovery in the near future. I want to say very frankly and directly that I believe that most of the published accounts in America during the last few years (whether by American or European observers) have been much too pessimistic. I have already referred to some of the mistaken fears which have partly accounted for what I believe to be this undue pessimism. But I would like to refer to two other fallacies which I believe have vitiated many observers' conclusions. In the first place, there has often been a tendency to take foreign exchange and currency variations as an index of economic development. The movements of the exchanges are the most obvious and clearly visible of economic or financial phenomena. Their expression in precise arithmetic figures has presented an irresistible attraction to those who wish to portray the great complex, obscure, massive, and multitudinous movements of economic life, in a simple and vivid form. But they are entirely misleading. European currencies as a whole fell further from their original gold prewar values in 1923 than in 1922, and in 1924 than in 1923. But the conclusion that Europe has been falling back and not recovering would be wholly fallacious. Let me give two examples. Poland, in the years immediately succeeding the war, when the depreciation of her currency was to be measured by hundreds or thousands, was in a desperately impoverished state. In the last two years, when the depreciation has to be reckoned in millions, her economic life has by comparison been prosperous and even stable. The whole position of Austria is of course infinitely better now, when the currency has less than one fourteen-thousandth part of its prewar value, than it was when the ratio was one-thousandth. This is not, of course, to say that the process of depreciation can continue without disastrous results. Ultimately it would be destructive in its effects. Austria has stabilized, and Poland is doing so—in both cases at almost the last hour. But it does mean that the extent of depreciation is no measure of economic progress or retrogression. Depreciation is at certain stages a stimulant to economic activity; at a later stage a disastrous impediment; at no stage is it a *barometer*.

There is one even more fundamental error into which I think many economists have fallen. They have not allowed sufficiently for the adaptability of man. Aristotle prefaced his great work on Politics with the remark that "Man is a political or social animal." I would like to see every economist take as the motto of his work: "Man is an adaptable animal." And I would like him, before committing himself to any conclusion or prophecy, first to ask himself deliberately, "Have I allowed sufficiently for the adaptability of mankind?" In a million ways during the last few years, throughout the worst stricken regions of Europe, man has adjusted his habits, his methods, and his needs to his new environment, and in so doing has built up again the economic system from below. In Europe today there are millions alive who by any arithmetic calculation should have died of starvation long ago, in the first years after the war.

I believe, then, definitely that Europe is progressing and not falling back, and that, given peace and confidence in peace, the progress will continue. Let me repeat for a moment.

The late war did three things. It destroyed accumulated wealth; but this material destruction was small either in relation to the accumulated material capital of the past or to the world's power of current production, and therefore it did not reduce the world's total wealth except incidentally and to a relatively negligible extent. That is, in other words, it did not reduce materially the total wealth available for current consumption during, let us say, the next ten years—the total wealth produced and the total wealth consumed; and therefore the average standard of life of the population will not be less because of that. The existence of debts, either between people or between countries, means a certain redistribution of a part of that production. You may say, if you like, that debts do not constitute a reduction of the world's wealth, or you may say, if you like, that they figure on both sides of the account. What is to the taxpayer a reduction of his wealth is to the bondholder, who is also a taxpayer, a part of his income. This is one of the great delusions which have caused and which still cause pessimism. If it were indeed true that the total income of the world were less by the amount of the debts or the payment of interest upon debts, the world would indeed be in a desperate condition; but that is not so.

Secondly, it left debts which remain a burden on national finances; but such debts cannot reduce production—*i.e.*, the total wealth available for current consumption—they can only affect its distribution. It was fortunately a physical impossibility for the war to consume the wealth of the future. Happily, in the fundamental and material sense, posterity *cannot* be made to pay. Thirdly, the war deranged economic processes, but there is no reason why the derangement should be permanent. It might well have been, and after another great war probably would be. But this time we have turned the corner. The basic pillars of our economic structure have tottered, but they have not fallen. The root of the world's economic troubles now, as I have attempted to indicate, is not (as has often been thought) in its nature permanent and material. It is essentially temporary, and in a sense immaterial. It is not that nature's resources, or man's capacity to exploit them, are insufficient. It is that the system of supply and demand has been temporarily deranged. And in spite of the incubus of the reparation problem and all the difficulties of the last five years, there has, on the whole, already been real progress in restoring the adjustment. I believe firmly, and have consistently believed, that for several years the economic recovery of Europe, disguised and retarded by the fall and fluctuation of exchanges, disguised and retarded by the central problem of reparation, has been steadily progressing. One by one the worst fears of the post-armistice period have been proving unreal or exaggerated— the fear of general Bolshevism, of a general disinclination to work, of the permanent effects of the destruction of capital and credit, of inadequacy of producing power, of a shortage of raw materials or of transport by sea and land. (I mention only factors each of which at different stages has been thought to be and treated at official conferences as being the fundamental trouble.) The fact is that the economic life of Europe during these years has been steadily growing up *from below;* the individual worker has resumed his habits of work, the individual manufacturer and merchant, within first a narrow but soon a widening range, has renewed his trade connections. They have been impeded by difficulties of state finance and by official restrictions, but on the whole they have been making way against them. Above all, in the international sphere the impediments have been disastrous. But we have a better hope now than at any previous time that the greatest of them all is about to be removed. And even with this impediment the progress has been real.

Let me summarize briefly the actual progress accomplished. I may perhaps be allowed to state first the main results achieved through the League of Nations. The League has taken two of the countries of Europe whose conditions were most desperate—Austria and Hungary—and has secured for them a definite basis of financial stability and economic development. Austria's currency, until the autumn of 1922 almost the least stable outside Russia, has since then been the most stable of all, as stable as the dollar itself. In place of an impoverished dependence upon the charity of other countries, she has reached a stable and self-supporting prosperity. Hungary is well on upon the same road of progress. And in both cases financial reconstruction has been attended by political security. Peace and political security have been established in a central and crucial region of Europe. In place of a morass of depreciation, impoverishment, disorganization, and political insecurity we have established an island of order and stability and assured peace. Within a smaller range, and in a different form, the League is now assisting Greece in its most serious economic problem, the settlement of its million refugees (one in five of the entire population) in productive employment. To take minor cases, a stable currency in Danzig in place of the demoralized mark, an economically successful administration of the Saar Basin, the resumption of production and the termination of disorder in Upper Silesia (after the Allied Governments had for many months failed through other channels) have all been achieved through the League. In many respects, I may add, these previous models assisted the experts in the preparation of their scheme for Germany. And in addition to work in specific countries, the League has assisted the resumption of international trade by negotiations designed to simplify passport and customs formalities, and to facilitate international transport. But the League's direct work, considerable though it has been, is, as I have said, only part of a much greater effort of reconstruction throughout Europe, which has for the most part come, in one country after another, not by international action, not even largely by national action, but from *within* and *below*.

Outside the League's action, Poland has built a strong and prosperous economic life in spite of all the disturbance of its disorganized exchange—and she is now making a notable, and so far successful, attempt to obtain stability even in her finances. Even in Russia there seems now a slow building up from a lower economic level. Czechoslovakia has restored her finances and established an apparent stability. The north of Europe is generally sound. Even in Germany the durability and toughness of her economic life in the midst of apparently crushing difficulties have certainly astonished the economists' anticipations. That the Ruhr occupation did not cause greater havoc in countries so intimately connected with it as Holland, Czechoslovakia, and Switzerland, shows how strongly rooted and stable the economic life of these countries had become. The essential economic strength of France—and the limits which this strength enables her to set to her financial troubles when she cares to make the effort—is now well recognized. The economic position of Italy is obviously more stable. In Great Britain—dependent above all on external trade and therefore above all injured by impediments to international traffic—the position and the prospects are at least better than they have been for years. Once settle the great problem of German reparations—once remove that greatest single obstacle to recovery—once create a basis of certainty on which the statesmen and merchants and manufacturers of the world can build with confidence, and then I have no doubt that the world will rapidly approach a new equilibrium. It may not at once, perhaps, give to all classes and all countries the full measure of prosperity or the full measure of security enjoyed before the war. But there is every reason to hope and believe that at no distant time the previous level will not only be reached but passed. Already at least those worst fears of the post-armistice period, the fear that Western civilization was tottering and perhaps destined to fall, the fear that Europe was destined to fall to a permanently lower standard of life—these fears, I think I may say with confidence, have already passed. They will be to us in the future mere nightmares of a distant and horrible past—only, of course, to regain a terrible reality if the memory of the last Great War fails to save the world from another.

ECONOMIC CONFLICTS AS THE CAUSES OF WAR

I SHALL begin at once with a bold, and perhaps provocative, general statement. The causes of war throughout history may be conveniently grouped as dynastic, religious, political, and economic. Of these four main causes, I believe that for practical purposes the first two—the dynastic and religious—may be considered as a part of past history; that the importance of the third—the political—while still considerable, is destined to diminish; and that the fourth alone—the economic—will continue to constitute a serious menace to the peace of the world.

I am, of course, aware of the dangers of such distinctions and of such general statements. I do not for a moment mean to suggest that the causes of different wars in history can be assigned exclusively to one or the other of these four main classes. Even in definition the distinction is not easy, and in action all of the several motives are often combined and confused. If a man's motives are known only to himself and his Maker, and not always to himself, the impulses of the complex personality of a nation are even harder to discern and state with confidence. All four of these main causes have indeed been sometimes combined in leading a country to war. A monarch may commit an act of aggression against another country whose economic resources he covets, basing his claim upon hereditary family rights, inflaming the ardor of his subjects by an appeal to their religion, and taking as his occasion either an alleged affront to national prestige or the political griev-ances of an Irredentist minority. That is, you may find as a cause of a single war a complex of dynastic, economic, religious, and political motives.

But though these motives may be combined in action, it is, I think, useful to distinguish them for this reason. Their respective importance as elements in the situation threatening war varies very greatly at different stages of the world's history.

Let us look at them in turn for a moment.

In one sense it is of course true that economic causes are the earliest, as I believe they will be the last, cause of war. Early history consists of succes-sive waves of invasion by hardy barbarians into more fertile regions where previous invading hordes have founded a life of comparative luxury, comfort, and civilization. But as we come to periods in history in which the conflicts are normally between two or more organized and civilized states, the purely eco-nomic motive tends to become for a time a less im-portant, or at least a less obvious and conscious, mo-tive of war. Other causes—such as the first three of the four named above—dominate, or at least give the general aspect.

For the first of these causes—the dynastic—I will take as a simple illustration the classical case of the war against Troy and the explanation given it by Homer. Now, it may be true, as certain economic historians would have us believe, that the real mo-tive of the Greek attack upon Troy was a desire to capture a trade route through to the Black Sea. Per-sonally, I have little sympathy with such an expla-nation. I regard it as a piece of economic pedantry, or

at least as an historical anachronism. Homer is very
likely to be wrong in his facts, but he is not very likely
to be wrong in his atmosphere. And I feel it easier to
conceive Menelaus acting as an indignant and out-
raged husband than Agamemnon as a far-sighted
economic statesman leading his country to war
through a consideration of trade routes. The assault
upon Troy, if Homer's account of the cause is true,
is a simple illustration of the many dynastic considerations which throughout long periods of history
have led to war. Frequently, through the Middle
Ages, and at other periods, we find a king leading his
country to invade a foreign territory because of a
claim derived from royal marriage alliances. This, a
fruitful source of war in the past, we may perhaps
now say with confidence is a danger unlikely to
threaten us in the future. Never again will a Louis
XIV, appearing dramatically in the Hall of Mirrors
at Versailles, announce: *"Il n'y a pas de Pyrénées,"*
and launch a War of the Spanish Succession. Never
again will a Henry V invade France to enforce a
claim derived from a table of royal pedigree. And we
have traveled far, even in the short space of the last
few years, since the militant forces of the world
seemed to find their expression and incarnation in a
monarch "in shining armor." It is not long in time,
but how far indeed in historical development, since
an English statesman could express his fear and suspicion of royal marriage connections, because if the
marriage was happy, the interests of his country
were likely to be sacrificed, and if the marriage were
unhappy, its friendly foreign relations likely to be
endangered. The militant monarchs of the world
have now retired to rustic obscurity, where they cul-

tivate their gardens and open bazaars. Those that remain in their offices represent the wishes of their inhabitants, and no longer either force or cajole them into a military aggression which they do not themselves desire. Wars have at least ceased to be the family affairs of monarchs.

And if the dynastic causes of war may be considered a part of the past, we may, perhaps, if we are looking to the reasonable probabilities of the future, also dismiss religious differences and the passions arising from them from among the serious menaces to peace. It is true, indeed, that in certain areas of the world—Ireland, for example—religious passions add a further poison to political differences. It is true that on the fringes and outskirts of civilization, we may still find a wave of fanatic savagery beating sometimes against the bulwarks of the West. But never again in any future which we can reasonably foresee need we expect that the great countries of Christian Europe will destroy each other to impose their respective religious creeds upon others; whether the conflict be on the medieval subtleties of theology that convulsed the Middle Ages, or the graver and more fundamental differences which led to the religious wars of the period of the Reformation. Men will fight no more to achieve for other men an eternal salvation which they do not want, or prefer to seek in another world.

I come now to the third cause—the political— which of course requires more serious consideration before we dismiss it as not likely to be a menace to peace equal to economic conflicts. "Political" is a wide and vague term. I intend to include within it both that group of ideas which centers about such

terms as "national pride" and "national prestige";
and also the desire of peoples to be governed by men
of their own race, rather than by aliens. Let me speak
for a moment of the first. The word "honor" has, I
think, rarely been more abused than it is when nations rattle their swords in the scabbard at the least
hint of what is too lightly called an "affront" to
national honor or prestige. It is one of the great steps
of progress marked by the League of Nations that it
does not except, as so many earlier treaties of arbitration did, questions affecting national honor from
those which can properly be discussed by an international tribunal. The stage marked by many of the
ideas and passions which circle around such phrases
as "national honor" is the same in international
affairs as was represented by the practice of dueling
in personal relations. It is no longer inconsistent
with the honor of a gentleman that he should settle
his differences before a civil tribunal, if he cannot
otherwise settle them without bloodshed. It may be
hoped that we shall soon reach the same stage in
international morality. In passing, I may, perhaps,
remark upon one likeness between the conceptions of
honor that were associated with the period of dueling and some present conceptions of national honor.
Honor, in the period of dueling, was often thought to
be the peculiar prerogative of a gentleman. His servant was not expected to possess it. A different view
is often taken by a great nation of what constitutes
an affront to its national honor, if the affront comes
from a small country against whom force can be
used with impunity. National honor is often too expensive a luxury for a small country, just as per-

sonal honor in the days of dueling was a luxury too
expensive for a servant.

But I come now to the more durable and, I think,
more laudable element in what I may call the political
causes of possible war—that is, the strong racial and
national feeling of different peoples, their legitimate
desire to be governed by those of like race or nation,
and too frequently their less legitimate desire to
oppress or dominate those of other races. This general group of sentimental feelings and aspirations is
undoubtedly among the most important factors to be
considered at the present moment by those who are
concerned with establishing such a system in Europe
as will conduce to a stable peace. In every part of
Europe in which trouble threatens, feelings of national hatred or national aspiration or national patriotism occupy the forefront of the minds of those
who are either threatening trouble or attempting to
avert it. At this moment sentiments and feelings of
this kind are so strong as in many cases to dominate
and obscure economic motives and considerations. I
believe, however, that in the importance which it now
possesses this is a temporary factor which, as a possible menace to peace, will diminish as the time
passes. During the war every combatant nation had
to exploit, develop, and inflame national patriotism
into national passion, in order to secure the motive
power required for a vigorous prosecution of the
war. These inflamed sensibilities and inflamed passions, together with, in some cases, suddenly revived
national aspirations after centuries of oppression,
remain as a major difficulty in the maintenance of
peace at present. But the inflamed condition of these
sentiments—not, of course, the sentiments them-

selves—derives from a temporary cause, and is likely itself to be temporary. In time the overacute consciousness of nationality will, I think, tend to diminish.

May I at this stage interpolate a reference to the extremely interesting theory which my friend, M. Aubert, is developing in his series of lectures, as to the relation between political and economic factors in the present problem of the settlement of Europe? I am not sure that I entirely agree with the distinction as he makes it, or with some of the conclusions which I think he draws from it. I do, indeed, agree that political factors are at the present time to an abnormal extent an element in the problem of European peace. I agree with him that to have attempted to override these political facts by policies determined solely by economic considerations would have been to cause explosions fatal to peace. I agree with him that many economists somewhat exaggerated the economic disadvantages entailed by some of the political provisions of the Treaty, and underestimated the extent to which economic conditions would in time adapt themselves to frontiers and other arrangements, based upon political rather than economic facts. Further than that, however, I cannot go. I think that it is not wise in any of the problems with which we have to deal in Europe, to base our scheme solely on political facts, and leave the economic life of the Continent to adapt itself thereto. I entirely agree with his description of fact, and of what happened, for example, in Upper Silesia, in Austria, and in Hungary; but the conclusion I draw is not that the primacy of political and the exclusion or the subordination of economic considerations should be

the basis of settlement. I think the true moral is that
in the actual state of Europe no settlement is really
satisfactory unless at one and the same time it takes
due account of both sets of considerations, and in-
cludes a political and an economic arrangement as
counterparts of one scheme. Let me illustrate. It is
true, I think, that in the conditions in which the
Upper Silesian problem was given to the League, the
League rightly drew its frontier with reference to
the political aspirations of its inhabitants, as expressed in the plebiscite. I agree that if economic
considerations had at that stage of the problem been
allowed to prevail completely, political trouble would
probably have broken the settlement. It is, however,
equally true, I think, that if the League had confined
itself, as the Conference of Ambassadors had been
thinking of doing, to drawing a frontier along the
plebiscite line, economic chaos and disaster would
no less certainly and disastrously have broken the
settlement. The essence of the League settlement of
Upper Silesia is that it included provisions destined
to give satisfaction at once to political aspirations
and economic necessities. So, too, in the League
schemes for the reconstruction of Austria and Hungary. A political protocol and an economic protocol
are essential counterparts, the one of the other; and
if in Upper Silesia the political arrangement perhaps
took the prior place, in the case of Hungary and
Austria the major basis of the scheme was economic
and financial.

I think, then, that while political and economic
factors are both of primary importance at the present moment in determining the chances of peace or
war, the political are likely to diminish, and the eco-

nomic, if anything, to increase in importance. Let us for a moment look at the state of the world from this point of view. While most, or many, of the actual disputes which have threatened the peace in Europe during these last few years wear at first sight a political rather than an economic aspect, we have only as a rule to look closely to see the economic element. Take, for example, a single natural resource, such as coal. Consider such a list of names of the regions of Europe as the Ruhr, Northern France, Upper Silesia, Teschen, the Pécs Mines. All these places are among the few coal-producing areas of Europe. Does not every one of them revive a vivid memory of disputes menacing peace? I scarcely dare turn from coal to oil, now the most dangerous word in our vocabulary; still less, to mention the names of those regions of the earth in which oil has been found, or alleged to be found, or is expected to be found. A mere whisper of the word may be enough to threaten the fate of an international conference. The modern "apple of discord" is a "tin of petrol."

Let me, however, hastily turn to more general considerations and a wider outlook. If we are anxious that the policy of the world should so develop as to maintain permanent peace, what is the ultimate difficulty, the ultimate problem? Surely it is this: If the final arbitrament of the sword is dispensed with, the tendency must be not indeed to stereotype absolutely, but to render less changeable, existing frontiers; to strengthen the *status quo* of the administrative and governmental divisions of the world. How can this be permanently consistent with the inevitable rise and fall of different nations in relative size and strength?

In the fifteenth century Spain was a great and

virile country and had an empire corresponding with her strength. In the sixteenth century Spain declined and France developed, and under the old system France acquired by force of arms an empire corresponding with her new strength. We have, more recently, had the great confederation of the United States, the British Empire, and the German Empire. The problem of adjusting the government of the world to such developments and declines in the relative strength of different nations will, perhaps, prove the supreme difficulty of any international policy designed to replace force of arms by peaceful settlement.

Obviously I cannot discuss this ultimate problem at length. May I, however, suggest that success or failure will largely depend upon whether it proves possible to drain some of their content from the passions behind national feeling? And here the crucial point will be, whether it is possible to isolate questions of commercial interest and advantage, and eliminate national feeling from them.

It is not beyond hope that if this can be done, the question as to which country shall govern some part of the territory of the world, while still engaging a perfectly genuine national sentiment, will not arouse this sentiment to a point at which a solution without force will be impossible. There may, for example, be a strong, legitimate, and laudable patriotism as between the inhabitants of two contiguous states in this country. But the frontier between them is no economic barrier. It does not affect the daily conditions of life and work of those on either side. There may be disputes and considerable feeling, but (with no great economic issue) they will not develop to the point of making the inhabitants of one side of the line wish to kill those on the other. It is possible to conceive a similar state of affairs with regard to national divisions of territory if there is not added to the genuine national feeling the much more dangerous element of competitive commercial interests. The more, however, the power of government is associated with the practice of using that power as an active and decisive factor in the competitive struggles of the world, the more there must be danger. If, for example, a particular country entrusts the valuable monopoly of a colony to a national trading company, the time will come when that company will, under the enervating influence of its special protection, serve both the exploiting country and the rest of the world inadequately and unfairly. In the long run, the world will not, and perhaps ought not to, tolerate the situation. This is only a single example of a principle which permeates the whole problem.

National passions may subside; national differences may diminish; the political causes of conflict may become as obsolete as the dynastic and the religious. But the economic effort of man—and the dangers of conflict which arise therefrom—is surely an immutable fact in any future we can foresee. New natural resources may be found and new inventions to exploit them, but not more quickly than the increase in population and the development of man's needs and desires. Always, so far as we can see, man throughout the world will be striving, struggling, competing, to improve his standards of existence. We do not point to a solution, we merely ignore the problem if we talk of replacing competition by coöperation. Coöperate we may in a thousand ways, nationally and internationally; and in so doing we may lessen the danger of competition, and direct its channels. But always in any future we can look forward to, we must accept in one form or another this fundamental fact of competitive economic struggle, national or collective. And the force so engendered is perhaps the strongest in the world. How is the policy of the world to be directed so that this irresistible natural force does not burst, explode, destroy? (If in what follows I express certain opinions on controversial questions, please remember that I speak personally, not as an official, and that I represent no one.)

In the most general terms, surely the only policy is a policy of safety valves. Or, to change the metaphor, if we attempt to restrain, to dam, to dyke the great tides of economic force, they will inevitably overflow, burst through, and spread ruin and havoc. The only policy is to draw the sluices, to open channels through which they may flow freely.

Let us look briefly and generally at some of the most probable causes of economic conflict. First, there are the troubles that arise about immigration, emigration, and surplus populations. What exactly is this danger? It is not that the world is now, or is in sight of being, inadequate for its inhabitants. It may indeed be that in a very distant and a very doubtful future, the resources of the world will be insufficient for an increased world population. But how remote that time is! How many things may defer it, may prevent it; the discovery of new national resources; the invention of new means of exploiting them intensively; a natural fall in the birth rates, or deliberate restriction, pestilences, or other causes.

And even without any of these, the day is remote.
The problem that will confront us, our sons, and our
grandsons is not a surplus world population—but
local surpluses in a world which still has immense
unexploited or half-exploited resources. This is a
problem that may cause wars but is essentially solu-
ble without them. Neither war nor the transfer of
territory from one country to another is necessary.
When Germany, for example, had a large colonial
empire it was not mainly to her empire that her emi-
grants went; the majority went to a country which
offered them a life of equal rights and equal opportunities under another flag. Since the war new restrictions, often for obvious and sufficient reasons,
have been imposed by many countries. But surely,
if we mean peace, we shall be able, either by separate
action or international arrangement, to find sufficient
outlets somewhere in the world among the still immense and half-developed areas, for a few "blocks"
of surplus population before the pressure bursts into
war.

Then there are the sets of problems centering
round raw materials. Some countries possess a very
advantageous proportion of the main natural resources of the world, which the rest of the world
need as the basis of their industrial and economic
life. Here again it is the policy of the countries in
question which will ultimately determine peace or
war. The geographical location of raw materials, or
the frontier within which they are included, need not
cause conflict—so long as they are available on equal
terms to the whole world. Conversely, a continuous
development of national policies in the direction of
cornering and exploiting these raw materials of the

whole world's industry, and for this purpose using the power of government, with the power of armed force behind, obviously points ultimately to war.

Closely connected with this is the semipolitical, semieconomic exploitation of backward areas of the world by the Great Powers. Perhaps the most dangerous part of this phase of the world's development passed in the nineteenth century—but obviously dangers remain. Here again the way of the danger is monopolistic and preferential exploitation—and the way of safety equality of treatment. I may here perhaps call attention to the immense importance of the principle embodied in the Covenant, and now enforced through the League, as regards the mandates over colonies of the Central African type. The mandatory power is to "secure equal opportunities for the trade and commerce of the members of the League"—which in practice means of all countries in the world. Consider how immense a potential danger of war will be avoided by the application of this principle; still more, if it is extended beyond the areas in which the Covenant makes it obligatory.

I confess that from the point of view of the peace of the world, the close association of the power of government with the competitive economic struggle seems to me to involve danger in innumerable ways; and the closer the association the greater the danger. I am not referring to ordinary tariffs or ordinary measures of nationalization. But if tariffs become discriminatory as a counterpart of general foreign policy; if an armed state enters actively the open arena of the international competitive struggle, the dangers to peace may be averted—but it is idle to ignore that they exist. It is a primitive and dangerous form of commerce when the trader goes with his goods in one hand and a pistol in the other. It may in time be regarded as a primitive and dangerous form of international relations for an armed state to be visibly at the elbow of its nationals in their competitive trade in foreign markets.

As one illustration of this, let me ask those of you who have studied political conditions in the smaller countries of Europe whether you were not sometimes taught that the mixed political and economic activities of the representatives of the Great Powers is a dangerous and disturbing factor in the local politics of the small country in which they are working.

I have suggested that too close an identification of the foreign trade of a country with its political power constitutes a danger to peace. But, indeed, I think in every human interest and activity an over-centralized, overnationalized system is undesirable from the point of view of peace and security in the world. It is not good that a writer or a scientist or a man should think of himself primarily as an American or an Englishman or a Frenchman. It is better for him as a scientist to think of himself as one of the scientists of the world, or, as a writer, as one of the writers of the world.

The more the activities of the world come into touch with each other not by contact at national frontiers but by cutting across them, the broader will be the basis of peace. Whenever the citizens of different countries meet on a basis of common interest that transcends and cuts across national frontiers—whether they are scientists or schoolmasters or business men or financiers, or trade unionists— whenever organizations develop on lines determined by their special purposes—science, education, business, finance, or labor conditions—and draw their members indifferently from every country, the basis of international relations is broadened and international amity no longer rests precariously on purely political foundation.

Here, however, I enter too wide a field of speculation. Let me return to ask whether in the public opinion of the world, and in the slow and gradual development of world policies, we can discern any indications of progress in the direction which means peace. I think we can. Let me hurriedly mention a few. I have already referred to the very important provision of the Treaty as to equality of opportunities for trade and commerce in mandate areas of the Central African type.

Let me add the provision of Article 23 of the Covenant requiring Member States to make provision to secure and maintain freedom of communication and of transit and equitable treatment for the commerce of all nations belonging to the League. Slow and gradual but real progress is being made by successive League conferences and conventions to translate these principles into practice. Then here is the provision in Article 12 of the Treaty of Versailles for securing free and equal terms of transit over four of the main rivers and certain of the great railroads of Europe, and you have the subsequent League Conventions and Agreements giving practical effect to these provisions. You have again, in numerous parts of the Treaty, provisions to open a channel to the sea to countries whose political frontiers do not give it. You have a general recognition, in numerous treaties, of the principle that the main channels of world communication should be open equally to all countries, irrespective of political administration. Behind these you have such general doctrines as the "open door"; or as the general principle in the third of the Fourteen Points (which is indeed far from being translated fully into practice but remains as a standard of policy which is likely to guide policy and direct opinion)—"the removal of all economic barriers and the establishment of an equality of trade conditions among all the nations consenting to the peace."

Here, surely, in these provisions, in these declarations, we have the hints, the indications, perhaps the prospect of a development of world policy, and of the recognized code of international practice which may rob economic conflicts of their sting; which may enable the secular economic struggle to continue without involving in it the armed forces of the world.

Let me, in conclusion, summarize the general substance of these chapters in a few sentences.

I look forward to the time when, in the words of George Washington, "commercial policy will hold an equal and impartial hand, neither seeking nor granting exclusive favors and preferences"; when, in the words of President Wilson, "economic barriers will be removed and 'equality of trade conditions' between nations be established"; when, in the phrase of the Covenant, "equitable treatment" will be secured in its fullest and most liberal sense; when the economic effort and competition of the world will pursue its way, neither expecting aid nor fearing hindrance, from governments holding the power of the sword in their land; when, in a word, there will be sufficient safety valves to rob economic forces of their explosive force. If world policy so develops, the problem of securing and maintaining peace will be practicable. But if world policy takes a different turn, if we find the great governments of the world bringing more and more the power, or the menace, of their armed force into the arena of economic competition; by this power pushing the trade of their own nationals and breaking that of others, blocking with dams and dykes and barriers the currents of the world's economic forces—sooner or later war must come. No system of arbitration, or conciliation, or of settling disputes at the point where they already threaten the peace, will stand the strain. The flood will burst its bounds and sweep our complex and precarious civilization into irreparable ruin.